NEW **Angling Mail**

GUIDE TO

COARSE FISHING

DAVE COSTER

Consultant editor ROY WESTWOOD

HAMLYN

Acknowledgements

The author and editor would like to thank the following fishery managers for their help in shooting the pictures for this book: Jack Ashford, Peter Cockwill, Ron Felton, John Raison, Graham Rowles, Dennis Smale.

All photographs by Roy Westwood.

First published in 1988 by
The Hamlyn Publishing Group Limited,
a Division of The Octopus Publishing Group plc,
Michelin House, 81 Fulham Road,
London SW3 6RB.

ISBN 0 600 55661 1

Printed in Spain

Contents

Basic principles 6

Getting started 6
Types of angler 8
Licences 9
Changing seasons 9
Permits 10
Day ticket waters 10
Club waters 11
Association waters 11
Private waters 11
The complete outfit 12
What the tackle box contains 14
Odds and sods drawer 15
Floats 16

Non-toxic weights 18

Substitues offer many benefits 18
Balancing the tackle 18
Floatfishing 19
Split-shot sizes 19
The leger 19
Performance ratings 19
Non-toxic weights 20
The top six substitutes 20
Carry a mixture 25
Non-toxic leger weights 25
The pole 26
Non-toxic pole weights 26
How they weigh up against lead 29

Floats 30

Line strength factors 30
Choosing the right float 30
Wagglers 33
Balsas 34
The right rod 35
Ring types 37
Reel seats and handles 37
The right reel 37
Closed-face confusion 40
The right line 41
Colour factors 41
Sinkers and floaters 42
The right hook 42
Putting it all together 44

Rigs and specials 46

River rigs and how to use them 47
Stickfloats 47
Medium paced water 48
Faster water 48
Balsas and Avons 49
Lake rigs 50
Close-range lake rigs 50
Middle distance and long range 51
Special floats 54
Canal Greys 54
Sliders 55

Attractors 56

The chief hookbaits 56
Maggot types 56
Improving shop maggots 57
Flavourings for maggots 58
Mounting maggots on a hook 58
Keeping casters fresh 58
Versatile bread 59
Worms 61
Seed baits 61
Hemp and tares 61
Sweetcorn 63
Boilies 63
Groundbait mixes 64
Pick of the Continental mixes 65
Catapults 66
Bait chart 67

Legering 68

Open-ended swimfeeders 68
Blockend feeders 69
Bite detection 70
Quivertips 72
The bow method 72
Springtips 73
Butt indicators 74
Monkey climbers 75
The right rod 77
The right reel 78
Line 79
Putting it all together 79
River rigs 80
Lake rigs 81

On the lake 82

Net to the side 82
Putty plummet 83
Clean bottom 85
Better fish 88
Fish care and handling 89
Dithering bite 89
Buried in the weed 90

On the river 92

Marshy margins 92
Stopping the splash 93
Cloud of attraction 93
Tares turn them on 95

All about the pole 100

Flick tip or elastic? 101
Handling methods 101
Unshipping sections 101
Short or long? 102
Weights and floats 103
Styl-leads and micro-shot 103
Float factors 103
Cane or wire stem? 104
Surface float 105
Shotting patterns 105
Rivers 105
Canals 106
Lakes 106
Lines for the pole 107
How long a hooklength 108
Pole fishing accessories 108
The bloodworm phenomenon 109
Feeding on the pole 110
Weight comparison chart 110

Index 111

BASIC PRINCIPLES

Opposite: The first fish of the morning lies securely in the landing net and the challenge now is how to keep them coming.

Coarse fishing has been revolutionised in the 1980s by a surge of technical advancements in tackle and techniques. Materials such as carbon fibre, kevlar and boron allied to skilful engineering and innovative design have improved the angler's basic equipment beyond recognition. The pace of change has embraced every single item from the smallest accessory, generating wholesale improvements in performance that are limited only by the angler's ability and, of course, the mood of the fish. Sometimes they get surly and then all the hi-tech gear in the world won't buy a bite!

More anglers are now specialising in single species, most notably carp, pike and barbel. In recognition of this trend, tackle has been purpose designed to the point where it's possible for a newcomer to obtain a standard specialist outfit, buy ready-made baits off the shelf and then strike almost immediate success by copying other more experienced anglers around him.

Fishing is no longer a hit and miss affair. There are now advanced tackle and baits to catch fish by design. But, if no great skill or knowledge is demanded, is there a danger of anglers becoming an army of bankside robots? The answer is most emphatically no! For evidence you need look no further than today's top anglers. Almost without exception the qualities that set them apart are dedication and a willingness to adapt continually to new ideas. Consistent success in coarse fishing must be worked for. It cannot be bought over the tackle shop counter and the angler who is slave to a single method will ultimately get left behind.

Apart from the satisfaction of catching 'good' fish, there are other rewards in this great sport. Hours spent by the waterside inspire respect for Nature. That's why so many anglers regard themselves as conservationists and defenders of the environment.

Getting started

Before setting out on the path of specialisation or trying to make your mark in any sphere of fishing, you must first get a grasp of the basic principles. Understanding how to go about locating fish then finding the best possible means of presenting the bait is the cornerstone of successful coarse fishing. That's where this book will prove invaluable. The essential lessons are here to help you gain the confidence to tackle any river or lake with a reasonable expectation of catching fish. Many of the methods described in the following pages owe much to matchfishing which has pioneered the lion's share of improvements in tackle and techniques.

Essentially, the objective is to help you obtain the best result from any swim. Once the fundamentals have been

A 4 lb tench — the class of fish that's comfortably within reach of all anglers once the fundamentals have been mastered.

The mirror carp with its scattering of large scales. This species has inspired generations of anglers because of its bulk and powerful fighting abilities.

mastered a much clearer perspective will emerge of the challenges the sport has to offer. There's little to be learnt from blindly slinging out a ready-made bait — or boilie as many specialist offerings are now called — and sitting back to await results. That's static, mechanical fishing and is not the correct way to start out.

Types of angler

The amount of time you can devote to fishing may well dictate the type of angler you will become. Most anglers fall into one of the following categories.

Pleasure

The term 'pleasure angler' is a loose definition but it adequately describes the person who fishes for the pure enjoyment of being by the waterside. This can include the man who snatches an hour's fishing after work or, just as aptly, the fanatic who fishes from daybreak to dusk. But broadly speaking the pleasure angler is the one who fishes his swim out for whatever may come along. He's just as pleased with 6lb of small roach as a brace of tench.

Club

Moving up the ladder we come to the club angler who takes his sport that bit more seriously. Many clubs organise regular outings which involve various competitions for the heaviest catch of the day or the best specimen fish. Club membership also offers the opportunity to rub shoulders with more experienced anglers, many of whom are prepared to share their knowledge at meetings and teach-ins. Joining a club is certainly the fastest way to learn the ropes and represents a good investment no matter what your age. And you'll discover kinds of new waters because club venues tend to be extremely varied.

Match

The match angler evolves from the club scene and is even more committed to the sport. Most clubs organise competitions themselves or enter teams in league events and the most consistent anglers on club outings soon find themselves selected. Then comes the temptation to progress into fishing the odd Open match where the demands are much greater. But beware! Match angling can be expensive and requires much more commitment to achieve success. Top matchmen can earn several thousand pounds in a season but expenses account for much of the winnings. It remains true that you cannot make a living from Open match fishing. The real satisfaction comes from competing and learning to catch fish under difficult conditions.

Normally you must draw for your swim — or peg as it is known — and contests are fished at the most demanding time of the day between 10am and 3pm when the sun is at its highest.

Specimen

Finally, there's the specimen angler who sets out to stalk target species which can vary according to the season. For example, tench are at their heaviest in June and July when they carry huge amounts of spawn and this is the peak period to seek a record fish. A specimen angler might start the season after tench, switching in the autumn to barbel or pike.

Meanwhile, some anglers stay loyal to the same species all season long. This is definitely the case with carp which have aroused virtually a cult following. At one time it was considered that carp remained dormant for most of the winter months but it is now quite common for exceptional specimens to be captured even in midwinter.

Fish like pike, carp, tench and barbel figure prominently in specimen hunting chiefly because they run big and are renowned for their fighting qualities. But the 1980s have seen bream, chub, roach and eels pursued with just as much vigour. This era of specialisation has pushed record fish weights way beyond the maximums considered possible just a few years ago. At one time, double-figure tench and 50lb carp seemed like an impossible dream but not any more!

Licences

All newcomers to the sport need documentation of some kind to fish legally. The country is split into ten water authority regions and each issues rod licences for its own area. You must obtain one of these wherever you fish, the income is then, theoretically, ploughed back into our river fisheries!

Before setting foot on any water with rod and line, check with your local tackle shop which authority licence is required. They can be bought to cover you for a full year or a shorter term if required. Average prices in 1988 range from £3 to £6 for an adult full season licence and £1.50 for a 10 to 14 day licence. There are usually concessionary rates for juniors, disabled anglers and pensioners.

Sadly, there's no such thing as a national licence so if you cross water authority boundaries you will need additional licences. It's important to appreciate that a rod licence confers no rights to actually fish unless the authority own a stretch of river and allow licence holders the freedom to come and go as they please. There are also limited free stretches on certain rivers where again a rod licence is sufficient but these free areas are the exception. You can only use one rod per licence although other rods may be tackled-up ready for action. If you want to fish with more than one rod then additional licences must be obtained.

If you want to tackle waters across a broad band of the country then you'll need a clutch of rod licences.

Changing seasons

The traditional coarse fishing season runs from June 16 to March 14 inclusive but this has gradually been eroded, in certain regions. Some authorities have scrapped

Coarse fishing is rarely predictable. One minute you can be straining to stop a big mouthed chub from dashing into underwater obstructions and the next whipping out a bristling young perch like the one shown here.

the Close Season completely while others allow landlocked waters to remain open all year round and limit the restrictions to rivers.

The Close Season was originally introduced to allow fish to spawn in peace and then recover from the rigours of spawning. But climatic conditions vary greatly from year-to-year and there's no guarantee that the fish will co-operate by spawning during the three month close-down.

Under fisheries legislation it's possible to amend the Close Season to try and coincide with peak spawning activity. It must be said that the fish do not appear to have suffered in areas where Close Season regulations have been relaxed and more widespread changes to the system are always possible. Your rod licence will carry full information about the seasons. If in any doubt consult your tackle dealer.

Permits

There are three possible routes to finding out if waters offer free fishing or are governed by the need to purchase day or season tickets.

The first, and easiest way, is to ask the local tackle dealer for names and addresses of club secretaries where permits can be obtained. Some tackle shops actually sell day tickets for local fisheries or offer a range of club books. The tackle shop is a good bet anyway because you're bound to get some extra advice on the baits and methods needed for a good day's sport in your particular area.

The second option is to write to the fisheries department of the local water authority. Several issue leaflets giving suggestions of where to fish in the region or clubs to contact. It is the clubs who are the lifeblood of fishing because they manage the majority of the waters in this country and you'll be surprised at the many miles of riverbank they have on their books. Support your local club because without them a great deal of our fishing could have been lost to other water users.

There are also commercially run clubs such as Amey Anglers and Leisure Sport with extensive gravel pit holdings.

The third way of investigating fishing waters is to actually visit the venue you fancy. There are normally noticeboards around the site giving details of where day tickets can be obtained. On canals, look for notices pinned to bridges.

Day ticket waters

There are two types of day ticket fishery: on some waters the bailiff issues tickets

Swan and angler share the same water space in harmony. That's the way it will remain.

on the bank, while on others the permit must be purchased in advance, normally from a tackle shop. Day tickets can work out expensive if you fish the same venue regularly. It may be cheaper to take out a season ticket.

Club waters

If a club leases or owns waters then membership automatically gains you a permit for these at inexpensive rates. Generally, club waters tend to be well stocked and managed. Joining normally simply involves writing to the secretary enclosing the required fee. Some clubs do sometimes have waiting lists but not often these days. Becoming a member of a club doesn't mean you must attend meetings or take an active part in its affairs although every crumb of extra support helps.

Association waters

The large angling associations with affiliated clubs boast extensive fishing rights. You can either join through a club which tends to be cheaper or as an individual. The membership book will give details of all the association's fisheries including maps and type of fish you can expect.

Private waters

These are often described as syndicate fisheries as they are frequently run by a group of individuals sharing the same interests who secure a lease on the fishing for their own private use. Payment of the lease is normally divided equally between the syndicate.

Personal contact is the key of the door to syndicates and if you're fortunate enough to gain a place it's normally the result of somebody dropping out.

Clubs are also formed specifically to gain the lease on a water that's in great demand because of the quality of its fishing and these tend to be more accessible although there is frequently a waiting list for membership.

Don't form the impression that the cream of the fishing lies in the hands of a privileged few. That is most certainly not the case. Most record fish over the years have been taken from waters open to the average angler.

THE COMPLETE OUTFIT

Here's the stockpile of tackle that Dave Coster has settled on for most of his fishing. It allows him to compete at the highest level in matchfishing or get maximum enjoyment from a pleasure session on a big fish water.

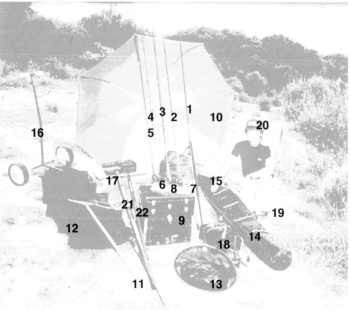

RODS see page 35.

1 13ft Daiwa carbon/kevlar match rod. Traditional three-piece with cork handle, hardened Dynaflo rings and finely tapering tip to take a range of different breaking strain lines. Generally used for long range waggler work and stick float fishing.

2 12ft Normark Microlite carbon match rod. Three-piece with cork handle but much softer through-action than the Daiwa 13-footer. Fitted with lightweight Fuji ceramic rings and used for light waggler and stick float fishing with fine lines and small hooks.

3 11ft 3in custom made, heavy duty swimfeeder rod. Carbon with ceramic rings and cork handle. It is made from a stiff actioned blank for punching out a feeder or big leger bomb a long way. There's a quivertip built-in which is made from solid carbon.

4 10ft custom-made, general purpose leger rod. Two-piece carbon with optional top sections: one takes three different actioned quivertips the other is for swingtipping.

5 7ft custom made, fibre glass wand. A short, soft through-actioned quivertip rod for delicate leger-ing work at close range.

REELS see page 37.

6 Ryobi Master match fixed spool reel. Lightweight carbon body with automatic bale arm for quick release of line. Good, general-purpose reel but mainly used for all forms of waggler fishing.

7 Mitchell Match fixed spool reel. Heavier and more robust than the Ryobi but with the same automatic, one touch bale arm. Now used by the author chiefly for swim feeder and leger fishing.

8 Daiwa Harrier closed-face reel. Wide diameter spool and made from graphite with a finger-dab line-release on the face. Mainly used for stick float fishing but also good for waggler work in windy conditions as this reel is almost tangle proof.

9 Continental style tackle seatbox. The base has lightweight aluminium sides which form a large compartment for carrying reels, groundbait and other bulky accessories. Adjustable legs are fitted to the base of the box so a comfortable sitting position can be maintained on awkward banks. The top half of the box is made from wood in four sections, comprising two pull-out tackle drawers and two lift-up trays.

10 Umberella with tilt mechanism, nylon coated, 100 percent waterproof Steadefast design. Essential part of the angler's equipment. The tilt comes in handy when the brolly is needed as a windbreak.

11 Assortment of bank sticks, some of which are extending types. Among the rod-rest heads note the distinctive Drennan quivertip design that allows the rod to be lined up at exactly the right angle.

12 Micromesh, knot-less 10ft keepnet. Built-in tilt mechanism for easy positioning. Keepnets have either round or square rings but many anglers are switching to the square variety because they offer more room for the fish when the net is staked in shallow margins.

13 Three-piece, fibre-glass telescopic landing net handle with pan type landing net head. The pan shape is favoured by match anglers because its shallow design makes fish removal and unhooking a great deal more easy and faster.

14 Rod carryall manufactured by Kevin Nash. This de-luxe match-man's model has two side pockets for umbrella and banksticks. Note the verti-cal zips for easy access. The main compartment holds up to eight rods and poles.

15 General purpose carryall. Originally designed for wet keepnets and landing nets. Now its chief use is to house various bait containers, flask, catapults and other bulky accessories as well as those wet nets in a side pocket.

16 Many anglers now use a trolley to help carry their tackle to the waterside if the terrain is suitable.

17 Bait waiter and bait boxes. This waiter is made from aluminium and takes several bait boxes or a groundbait mixing bowl. It can be positioned so the bait is easy to hand from a sitting or standing position.

18 Groundbait mixing bowl. Folds flat for easy storage.

19 Green, thigh length waders.

20 A cap with a substantial peak or an anti-glare visor takes the strain out of studying a float or bite indicator for many long hours.

21 Olympic Champion pole, 13.5 metres, made from high modulus carbon in take-apart sections. Very light, slim diameter model. There's a choice of three top sections which are fitted out with different grades of internal elastic shock absorber. It is used for all pole fishing beyond six metres and the different tips will deal with fish ranging from a few ounces to several pounds. Depending on the choice of tip section, lines from a delicate 5oz breaking strain up to 3lb can be used.

22 Kevin Ashurst carbon whip, 6 metres in length. Part telescopic and the rest take-apart sections. Bottom three sections have been modified to break down for shallow canal swims. Another light pole with an extremely fine flicktip to compensate for light breaking strain lines. No shock absorber system is fitted to this model. Often used as a backup to the Olympic when a secondary shorter line is being fished under match conditions. Basically for small fish when speed fishing to hand at distances up to seven or eight metres.

WHAT THE TACKLE BOX CONTAINS

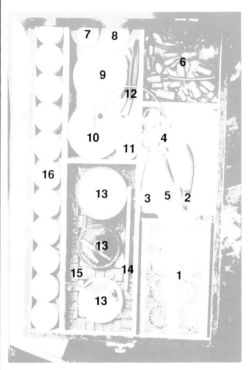

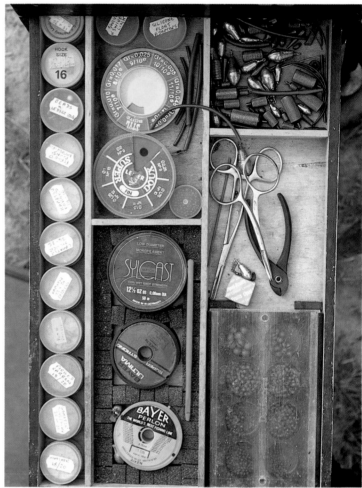

1 Sliding-top container of mixed Sandvik and Dinsmore non-toxic shot in sizes from SSG down to No. 8s. (See page 22.)

2 Shot pliers made from soft plastic to use with fragile Sandvik weights.

3 Forceps. Useful for un-hooking fish, also for fine tackle adjustments like snipping the barb off hooks.

4 Scissors. Make sure they are small and sharp.

5 Non-toxic Arlesey-bomb. (See page 25.)

6 Selection of non-toxic Screwbombs and Snapshot Arlesey bombs. Also silicone tubing in uncut lengths used for making bomb and feeder links. (See page 25.)

7 Swivels and swivel links. (See page 26.)

8 Silicone quick-change float adaptors. (See page 51.)

9 Container of Styl leads in legal sizes from No.7-12. (See page 26.)

10 Container of micro shot from No.8-12 for fine hooklengths. (See page 28.)

11 Dinsmore No.8 shot. (See page 22.)

12 Feeder links, some fitted with Power-gum. (See page 68.)

13 Sylcast, Ultima and Bayer hooklength lines in strengths from 12oz to 1.7lb. (See page 41.)

14 Disgorger. (See page 98.)

15 Plummets. (See page 83.)

16 Pots of hooks rang-ing from No.6s down to 26s. Patterns include fine wire, forged, spade-end and eyed. These types of hooks are used for fishing a variety of baits including hemp, tares, maggots, blood-worm and bread.(See Attractors page 56.)

ODDS AND SODS DRAWER

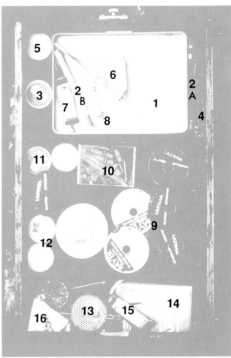

1 Breadpunch board.
(See page 60.)

2 Breadpunches with multi-heads for different hook sizes.
(See page 60.)

3 Small diameter float-silicone.

4 Disgorgers.
(See page 98.)

5 Small eyed specimen hooks in sizes 14, 16 and 18. Used for tench fishing when small baits are needed.
(See page 44.)

6 Styl pinchers.
(See page 22.)

7 Red Mystic paste. Synthetic bait which imitates bloodworm.
(See page 61.)

8 Packet of size 26 silver Gamakatsu hooks for fishing squatts on hard canal venues.

9 Selection of hook-length lines, Bayer Ultima fine diameter nylon and standard Bayer ranging from 1.1lb to 4.6lb.
(See page 41.)

10 Cut lengths of Sandvik tungsten-tube for locking big wagglers in SSG and AAA sizes.

11 Large diameter float silicone for top attachment on stick floats.

12 Various hookpots.
(See page 42.)

13 Bait droppers. Mainly used with pole. (See page 110.)

14 Wallet of licences.
(See page 9.)

15 Black Mystic paste to imitate hemp on the hook.

16 Mini Starlights for night fishing. Several uses for floats, quivertips and bobbins.

FLOATS

This is the comprehensive range of floats carried by Dave Coster to cover every eventuality. How and when they are used is covered in chapters three and four.

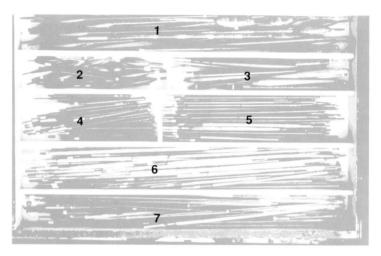

Wagglers

1 Large bodied wagglers for distance fishing up to 40 metres on lakes, gravel pits or reservoirs. Also, bodied, bottom-end sliders for deep stillwaters. (See page 33.)

2 These are not wagglers but nobody's box is perfect! They're big top and bottom attached balsas for fast, turbulent water and top and bottom sliders for deep, sluggish rivers. (See page 34.)

3 Short bottom-end, bodied wagglers called Trent Trotters which are intended for very shallow, fastish river swims. Plus an assortment of very short balsa floats for shallow streams. (See pages 49 and 51.)

4 Light wagglers with extra fine inserts for delicate canal presentation. These floats are up to 3BB loading only and will be used up to a maximum range of 15 metres. (See page 33.)

5 Even lighter, custom-made wagglers with longish, fine inserts for surface fishing or close-in presentation on-the-drop style.

6 Home-made, dyed sarkandas reed, insert wagglers from 3BB to 5BB. Chiefly for fishing tight up to the far bank of canals or small rivers. The large selection means a float carrying exactly the weight for spot-on, accurate casting can be selected.
(See page 33.)

7 Insert and straight Crystals for clear, shallow waters where a dark float could throw a shadow on the bottom and scare wary fish. The longer inserts carry up to 5AA and will help combat surface drift problems on stillwaters. Straights have more buoyant tips and are used for fishing the bait on the bottom when drift would drag under an Insert model. (See page 34.)

Sticks

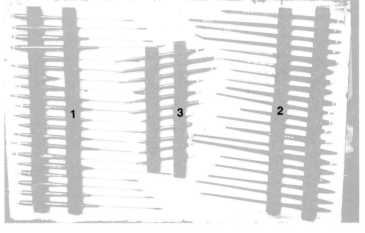

1 Wire stem stick floats with different types of top. Shown here are the pointed and the more traditional taper. The actual choice of float depends on the bait presentation required. Shot loadings range from just three No.8 dust-shot, up to eight No.4s. Generally this type of stick float is used on pacey rivers in depths ranging from 60cm to 2.5 metres (2 to 8ft). (See page 30.)

2 Conventional stick-floats with cane and lignum or straight plastic stems for medium paced river fishing. Again, there's a mixture of tip shapes. (See page 30.)

3 Smaller sticks and all-balsas for mid-water work or small stream fishing. (See page 34.)

NON-TOXIC WEIGHTS

Substitutes offer many benefits

The discovery that swans are susceptible to lead poisoning as a direct result of ingesting discarded leger weights and split-shot in mistake for bankside grit, caused the Government to very quickly introduce legislation banning the sale and import of specific sizes which it considered posed a threat.

Most water authorities followed suit and introduced local byelaws banning the same sizes outlawed by the Government.

Essentially, you cannot use any lead weights between 0.06 grams up to and including 28.35 grams (1oz). This embraces all lead split-shot from SSGs down to No.7s. Arlesey bombs and similar leger weights in the most popular sizes are also banned. The legislation also excludes lead Olivettes used by pole anglers.

In response to the elimination of these weights a new generation of non-toxic substitute weights made from materials like tungsten and tin have been developed which offer a great many benefits to the modern, conservation conscious angler. For the first time in the long history of the sport there are weights which have been purpose-designed for fishing. This book is the first to explain and assess the performance of the new, non-toxic split-shot. In this chapter you will find positive suggestions on how they can be used to best effect.

Balancing the tackle

Coarse fishing can be split into two distinct categories: floatfishing and legering. Both methods rely on some form of weighting to cast the bait out and to balance it in a way that attracts the fish to bite.

These weights are positively safe. All are non-toxic look-alikes of the traditional split-shot and perform in a very similar manner.

Floatfishing

The term floatfishing applies to any rig which uses a buoyant surface indicator to show up bites.

There are purpose-designed floats for canals, rivers, lakes and gravel pits. Floats for fishing close-in and at distance. And specialist floats for deep water and shallows. But there is not as yet a universal float to meet all these demands.

A floatfished bait can be presented anywhere from the surface through midwater to the bottom. It can also be given varying rates of descent to try and catch the fish's attention by looking either natural or just plain odd. Weights called split-shot balance the float and provide casting weight.

Split-shot sizes

Split-shot have been an integral part of floatfishing for many generations. Originally these weights were a by-product from the manufacture of shotgun cartridges. When cut centrally in their lead form, they proved ideal as fishing weights. The larger sizes were known as SSG, AAA and BB and the smaller shot numbered 1 to 8. The higher the number, the smaller the size and weight of split-shot.

This somewhat confusing classification has persisted through the change-over period to non-toxic replacements for lead. The modern substitutes made from tin, tungsten and secret compounds are almost all graded in the same way as lead.

The biggest weights like SSGs and AAAs are often described as **locking shot** when used to fix a bottom-end float, or waggler, on the line.

The middle sizes known as No.1s, 3s, 4s and 5s have a wealth of different applications. When any of these sizes are grouped together, they are popularly labelled as **bulk-shot**.

Small shot from No.6 to 8 are commonly used on the hooklength for very fine adjustments. The No.8s have become known as **dust-shot** because of their small size.

In more recent times, **micro-shot** have filtered into fishing — chiefly as a result of the explosion of interest in pole fishing which utilises a fixed line and extremely delicate rigs. Micro-shot run from No.9s down to ridiculously tiny No.15s.

The leger

It would be fair to say legering is less complicated and certainly less frantic than floatfishing. The float is discarded for a single weight, usually an **Arlesey bomb**, which even in its smallest size is much larger and heavier than a split-shot. The bomb is attached to the line by a swivel and anchors the bait firmly on the bottom.

Bites are registered by fitting various indicators to the rod like swingtips, quivertips, bobbins or electronic alarms. The leger is a good method when the float is found wanting because of bad weather, very fast currents or the fish being beyond the range of float tackle.

Performance ratings

☆Fair ☆☆Good ☆☆☆Excellent
Not recommended

Product	Light stick float	Heavy stick float	Locking light waggler	Locking heavy waggler	Waggler dropper shot	All balsa	Link leger	leger stop
Wimet Safeweights	☆☆	☆	☆☆☆	☆☆	☆	☆	☆☆☆	
Lockshot Match	☆	☆☆	☆☆☆	☆☆☆	☆	☆☆	☆☆☆	☆☆☆
Dinsmore Safe Shot	☆☆☆	☆☆☆	☆☆	☆☆	☆☆	☆☆☆	☆☆☆	☆☆
Metryk Supa Shot	☆☆	☆☆	☆☆☆	☆☆	☆	☆☆	☆☆	☆☆
Thamesly Sure Shot	☆☆	☆☆	☆☆	☆☆☆	☆	☆☆	☆☆☆	☆☆
Aiken Super Shot	☆☆	☆☆	☆☆☆	☆☆	☆☆	☆☆	☆☆	☆☆

Non-toxic weights

It is surely a credit to the ingenuity of anglers that we now have a whole range of replacement, non-toxic weights on the market in different sizes and materials.

After intensive evaluation, certain brands have inevitably emerged as the market leaders. The following are among the best.

Top six substitutes

Wimet Safeweights

Precision made from a tungsten and polymer mix with internal copper hinge. They are dark matt carbon in colour and slightly lighter than many rival brands but much smaller size for size. They are re-usable with care and in the larger sizes the thumbnail slot allows reopening for moving along the line. Safeweights are obtainable in all popular grades.

Tips The secret is not to open up Safeweights too far or the hinge weakens. The shot clicks shut on line under finger pressure — but don't slide it otherwise it will start to slip. Instead, reopen the Safeweight, reposition and close again. Smaller sizes are particularly fragile and will break up if too much force is applied. It's better to secure these on the line with plastic shot pincers which give a more even pressure. Never use your teeth!

●In SSG and AAA sizes, Safeweights secure well on the line but will fly off if they smack against a solid object such as far bank piling or a moored boat. A legal No.8 lead shot positioned above and below locking shot will help greatly here.

●Smaller hinged shot can slip or fly off with vigorous casting or striking. But they are less likely to slip if repositioned in two or threes, tight up to each other. Safeweights are extremely kind on nylon line and cause no visible damage.

Wimet Safeweights — tungsten and polymer mix with a copper hinge.

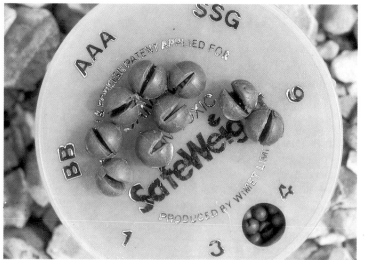

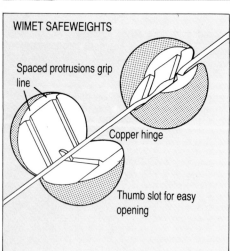

WIMET SAFEWEIGHTS

Spaced protrusions grip line

Copper hinge

Thumb slot for easy opening

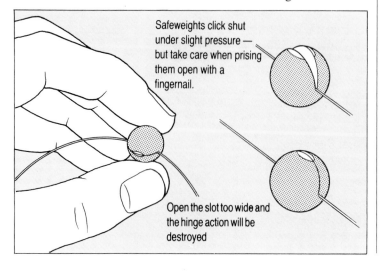

Safeweights click shut under slight pressure — but take care when prising them open with a fingernail.

Open the slot too wide and the hinge action will be destroyed

Metryk Supa Shot

A secret mixture of non-toxic alloys with a fingernail recess for easy reopening. The bright finish is dulled with a black coating which is reasonably permanent. They are re-useable and very robust.

A shade larger, size-for-size, than lead shot but they look remarkably similar. Metryk are available in sizes SSG, AAA, BB, No, 1, 4, 6 and 8.

Tips Easy to close in the smaller sizes but some batches of the bigger shot require considerable pressure to fix

on line. The cut is rather deep, if it was less severe Supa Shot would hang better on the line.

●Smaller sizes are kind on nylon and can be used with confidence on light breaking strains down to 1lb. Larger

Far left: Metryk Supa Shot, robust and re-useable.

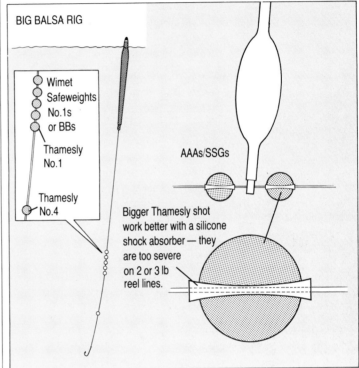

BIG BALSA RIG

Wimet Safeweights No.1s or BBs

Thamesly No.1

Thamesly No.4

AAAs/SSGs

Bigger Thamesly shot work better with a silicone shock absorber — they are too severe on 2 or 3 lb reel lines.

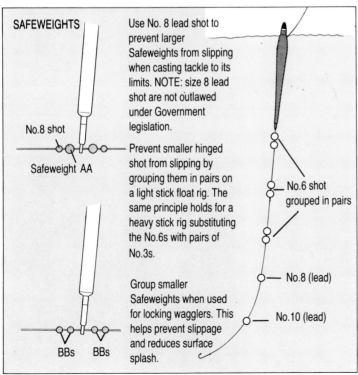

SAFEWEIGHTS

No.8 shot

Safeweight AA

BBs   BBs

Use No. 8 lead shot to prevent larger Safeweights from slipping when casting tackle to its limits. NOTE: size 8 lead shot are not outlawed under Government legislation.

Prevent smaller hinged shot from slipping by grouping them in pairs on a light stick float rig. The same principle holds for a heavy stick rig substituting the No.6s with pairs of No.3s.

Group smaller Safeweights when used for locking wagglers. This helps prevent slippage and reduces surface splash.

No.6 shot grouped in pairs

No.8 (lead)

No.10 (lead)

shot work well for locking wagglers. Unlike other products, there's no need for a protective sheathing of silicone around the line to protect it from the hardness or rough edges of the shot. They can be used as lockers on reel lines certainly down to 2lb. Middle and small sizes are fine for locking bigger Safeweights in position on waters where lead is totally banned.

●Metryk Supa Shot are good when teamed up with other non-toxic weights. They should fit the bill for many coarse anglers, particularly beginners as they are relatively easy to use. The deep cut is annoying but if you slip silicone rubber on line and pinch shot over this they'll hang a lot better. Smaller sizes can be positioned more centrally on line before closing.

●Unlike several other alternatives, it is possible to carefully trim off bits from these weights with a sharp pair of scissors. (See page 21.)

Dinsmore Safe Shot

Tin based with an excellent semi-permanent black finish. Larger sizes are very uniform. For example, 2BB equals 1AA precisely.

The smaller shot are not quite as well formed but the cut is less severe than other substitutes and they hang far better on the line. Approximately 80 percent weight equivalent when compared with lead of same size. Sizes are SSG, AAA, BB, No.1, 3, 4, 5, 6 and 8.

Tips Smaller Safe Shot are very easy to close with finger pressure and although bigger than lead they're probably the best substitute for stick float fishing.

Far right: Dinsmore Safe Shot — tin based with permanent black finish.

Below right: A Levapiombo helps move and remove shot.

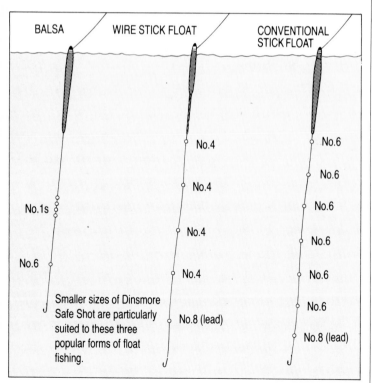

BALSA   WIRE STICK FLOAT   CONVENTIONAL STICK FLOAT

No.1s

No.6

Smaller sizes of Dinsmore Safe Shot are particularly suited to these three popular forms of float fishing.

No.4
No.4
No.4
No.4
No.8 (lead)

No.6
No.6
No.6
No.6
No.6
No.6
No.8 (lead)

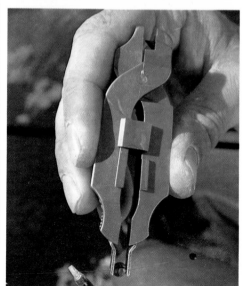

- No silicone buffer is needed to protect lines when using sizes 1 to 6. Larger BBs, AAAs and SSGs won't hang so centrally but the cut is still not as deep as other weights.

- Bigger shot are severe on light lines and they need a silicone buffer to avoid crack-offs on the strike.

- They are very difficult to open once nipped on fine lines. There's only a slight fingernail recess in the SSG size and all the other shot in the range close completely flush. It's a devil of a job to remove them if you don't use silicone as a line protector.

- One solution to this problem is to use a commercial shot remover and slider call a Levapiombo which is imported from Italy. With this handy device you can apply side pressure to the shot and move them easily to a new position.

Anglers Match Snapshot and Lockshot

Dense surgical plastic mixed with tungsten. They have a very dark colour with a matt finish. These weights come in two halves which push together after the 'male half' has been clipped on the line by its peg.

There's a groove for easy reopening with the fingernail and the sizes available are SSG, AAA, BB and No.1.

Tips With Lockshot Match, which are a more refined, heavier version of the original polyferic Lockshot, the line is placed over the peg on the male half and pulled down as far as possible. The cap is then added and squeezed tight to lock the line.

- To release, insert a fingernail into the groove that separates the two halves and twist off the cap. Never attempt to slide these shot along the line. It's virtually impossible without loosening the two halves beforehand. Lockshot are the most stable of the non-toxic alternatives yet they don't damage even fine lines. They also hang perfectly central and are superb as locking shot on wagglers, for link legers and as leger or feeder stops.

Aiken Super Shot

This is another alloy based material with a very uniform shape and easy-to-open fingernail recess. Almost identical to Metryk Supa Shot and works in similar fashion. It is reusable with a silvery finish which eventually dulls down. Sizes comprise SSG, AAA, BB, No, 1, 3, 4, 5, 6 and 8.

Tips Soft in smaller sizes and suitable for fine lines. The No.8s are particularly valuable for anglers fishing waters where there's a total ban on lead. SSG and AAA sizes can be severe and require silicone tubing buffer.

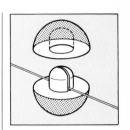

Lockshot

Far left: Anglers Match Snapshot offers two types of weight.

Left: Aiken Super Shot, soft in smaller sizes.

Smaller shot work well as lockers on small wagglers and for light stick floats as drop shot.

- Super Shot will cover many forms of fishing and are again ideal for the beginner. Excellent for locking light wagglers and for top and bottom attachment floatwork. The cut is a bit deep and shot tend to hang a little erratically. But you can position smaller sizes carefully before closing them on line for a better hang.

- Super Shot is soft enough to trim with sharp scissors but take care.

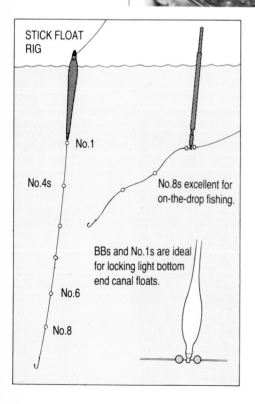

Thamesly Sure Shot, alloy based and uniform shape.

Thamesly Sure Shot

These are probably the toughest substitute weights on the market. They'll open and close repeatedly with no sign of weakening.

They are a good, spherical shape darkened down with graphite. Because of their unformity, Thamesly weights have become popular with match anglers who demand highly accurate shotting.

They're made from a hard mixture of alloys and a silicone buffer is recommended to cushion the larger sizes on the line. It's possible to carefully trim off pieces from larger SSG, AAA and BB sizes with scissors.

Tips The cut is rather deep but use the buffer as recommended with bigger shot and the weight will hang rather better. Thamesly make secure locking shot and legering links. Sizes 1, 4 and 6 are fine for certain forms of stick and balsa fishing. This brand is good as a stop for legers and swimfeeders.

- Sure Shot are a bit bulky and in the AAA and SSG sizes make a fair splash on touchdown when used as

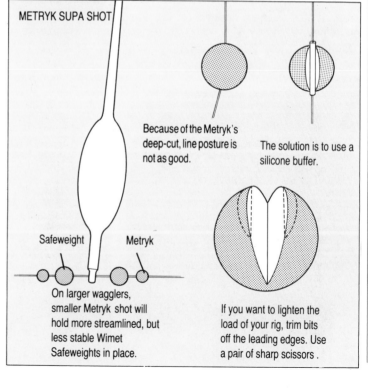

STICK FLOAT RIG

No.1

No.4s

No.8s excellent for on-the-drop fishing.

BBs and No.1s are ideal for locking light bottom end canal floats.

No.6

No.8

METRYK SUPA SHOT

Because of the Metryk's deep-cut, line posture is not as good.

The solution is to use a silicone buffer.

Safeweight   Metryk

On larger wagglers, smaller Metryk shot will hold more streamlined, but less stable Wimet Safeweights in place.

If you want to lighten the load of your rig, trim bits off the leading edges. Use a pair of sharp scissors .

lockers on big wagglers. The best solution is to change to a semi-loaded waggler or to fish with smaller BBs or No.1s in groups.

- But you'll find smaller shot difficult to use in bulked groupings as they hang awkwardly on line. Safeweights appear a better bet although you can finish off the line of shot with a more stable Thamesly underneath.

Carry a Mixture

Obviously it is impractical to carry all the substitute shot mentioned here, but a mixture is recommended because certain brands perform better for some functions than others. Remember that the objective always is to try and achieve the best possible presentation of the hookbait.

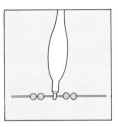

To help you make your choice of split-shot the floatfishing rigs in this book include descriptions of the actual brands used. But as an interim guide the Performance ratings (page 19) should prove helpful. The chart comparing the new substitute sizes with their lead equivalents demonstrates how close the manufacturers have come to producing exact copies of the old lead weights across the board.

Group smaller BBs or No.1s to lessen the splash when the float touches down.

Non-toxic leger weights

Screwbomb

The first non-toxic Arlesey bomb to reach the market was the Screwbomb made from blackened brass. As the name suggests, it has a screw-on top fitting which incorporates a swivel head. Once the swivel section is attached to the line, any of this range of weights running from one-eighth of an ounce up to one ounce can be fitted in seconds. That means you don't have to break down the rig to change up or down in weight size if conditions dictate a modification to your set-up. When any of the base units are fitted to the swivel attachment, the finished Screwbomb

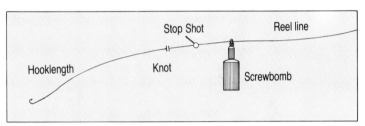

vaguely resembles the profile of a conventional Arlesey made from lead. In fact, it works better in flowing water because there is a slightly more pronounced step from the body to the swivel section and this results in the Screwbomb gripping the bottom more securely in strongish

The simplest, most uncluttered form of legering using a Screwbomb.

Non-toxic leger bombs come in all shapes and sizes.

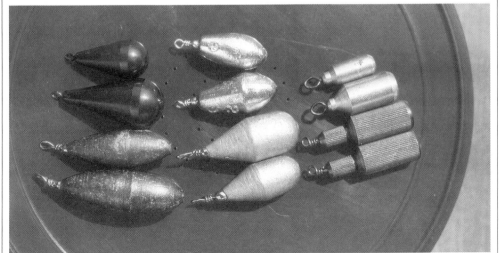

currents. Certainly, for uncluttered legering rigs this is the best form of weighting because the quick-change facility eliminates the need to rely on any other type of swivel or link for attachment to the line.

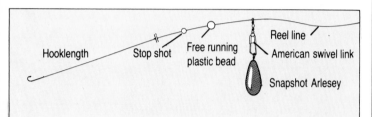

Hooklength   Stop shot   Free running plastic bead   Reel line   American swivel link   Snapshot Arlesey

Snapshot

The other new Arlesey which quickly arrived on the scene was the Snapshot model which at first glance looks exactly like its lead predecessors. It is made from a much harder, alloy-based material and will cover most legering requirements within the casting range of a three-quarter ounce bomb which is the heaviest weight in the series. It doesn't have the quick-change facility of the Screwbomb but being smaller, size-for-size, and more streamlined, its advantages outweigh this drawback.

Apart from sometimes finding a need to change leger weight size, it is also common to switch between a swimfeeder and Arlesey bomb several times during a session. The swimfeeder deposits loose offerings in the vicinity of the hookbait but can frighten the fish once they are drawn into the swim. So if a Snapshot Arlesey or Screwbomb is to be used in these circumstances it is best to make the tackle up with an American swivel-link running on

the line. This has a conventional swivel at one end and a quick-release attachment ate the other which can be unclipped to take any leger weight or swimfeeder.

The pole

Pole fishing has recently grown into something of a cult among both matchmen and pleasure anglers. The method had its origins on the Continent where countries like France and Italy developed this form of fishing without reels to the point where they began to dominate the world matchfishing arena.

In fact, it was due to the success of the Continentals in the World Championships that Britain's top internationals finally decided they had to take on the aces across the Channel at their own game.

The chief benefit of the pole is improved tackle presentation. Today we have lightweight carbon poles as long as 13 metres. Using a pole of that length you can fish incredibly light and sensitive rigs at distances that could never be reached using a traditional 13ft rod and running line. The pole tip can be positioned directly over the float so as to lift into the slightest indication of a bite.

Because the pole tip is usually only a couple of feet from the float, the tackle can be manipulated in many ways. For example, on rivers the bait can be held back against the current much further out than with a shorter rod and reel and on stillwaters it's possible to induce all kinds of bait movement to provoke bites.

Non-toxic pole weights

There are four recognised ways of weighting pole tackle. The first is with normal shot which have been covered earlier in this chapter. Then there are specialist Olivettes, Styl leads and micro-shot. The last two are still legal in lead because they are so small and don't present any problems for wildlife. But some fisheries ban the use of any size of lead.

Styl Leads

These are tiny elongated weights, shaped much like celery with a groove running down one side into which the line is inserted. They are fixed on the line with special pincers. The biggest legal size is a No.12 weighing less than 0.06 of a gram and they run through several sizes down to a No.7 scaling 0.010 of a gram. Their

Olivette with internal silicone buffer (approx X3).

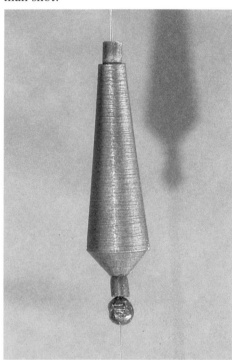

The Styl weight (approx X10).

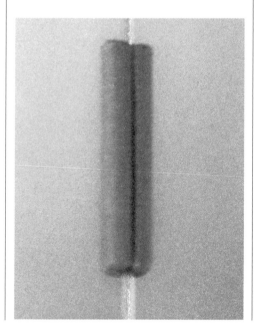

main benefit is that they give a much slower rate of descent to the end tackle than shot.

Micro-shot

These run from No.9s down to 15s which are so small you really need a magnifying glass to clip them on the line! But there's no real need to go that tiny. The No.10s and 11s are the most popular sizes for use on the hooklength when pole fishing. Like Styls, these weights fall slowly through the water and offer very delicate presentation. The fish almost seem oblivious to them because they're so small.

Olivettes

These are used when a bulk weight is needed for swinging a tackle out on the pole or when there's a need to get the hookbait down to the fish quickly in deeper water. It's also the first choice to hold the tackle stable in fast currents. This streamlined weight offers little resistance against flow and by concentrating most of a float's loading in one area helps keep rigs simple and tangle-free.

Non-toxic Olivettes vary in price. At the top end are the Streamline tungsten brand which although very expensive, are actually heavier size-for-size than the lead weights they replace. Then there are the DAM Milo set which are alloy coated in a coloured plastic. Each size is an easily recognisable different colour!

Several companies import alloy based Olivette weights from France which are very reasonably priced but they are significantly lighter than the Streamline and Milo versions.

Finally, an innovative design is the Snapshot Lock and Slide Olivette which unlike the other designs doesn't have a central hole for the line to pass through. Instead, there are protrusions at either end on which short lengths of silicone are fitted to strap the weight to the line. These weights are made from turned-down brass.

How they weigh up against lead

Size	Lead	Dinsmore	Aiken	Metryk	Wimet	Thamesly
SSG	1.68	1.60	1.68	1.60	1.70	1.62
AAA	0.75	0.80	0.85	0.90	0.76	0.82
BB	0.41	0.40	0.38	0.42	0.34	0.42
No.1	0.30	0.30	0.28	0.26	0.26	0.30
3	0.20	0.20	0.26	....	0.18	....
4	0.18	0.17	0.22	0.20	0.14	0.20
5	0.16	0.15	0.16	0.16	....	....
6	0.10	0.10	0.11	0.12	0.06	0.10
7	0.08	....	....	....	....	....
8	0.06	0.06	0.05	0.05	....	....

All weights recorded in grams on electronic scales by Dave Coster

FLOATS

The most exciting sight in fishing is a brightly coloured float tip diving out of sight into the murky depths. You're never completely certain what size or type of fish has grabbed the bait. The float's vanishing act is the climax of considerable preparation and anticipation — not to say unquenchable optimism!

If you can present the right bait at the right depth and make it behave in the right manner, learn efficient loose feeding or groundbaiting then all other things being equal you should catch fish — or at least tempt bites. When everything is brought together floatfishing can be the most satisfying method of catching fish.

The basic principles of floatfishing are really that simple, but remember the float has to be utilised to its maximum sensitivity. It needs to be weighed down with correctly positioned split-shot on the line until only the pointed sight tip remains visible. This is a fundamental technique known as **dotting the float**. The shot needs to be positioned carefully, particularly near the hook, to avoid spooking the fish.

Line strength factors

Lines are very important. Use too heavy a breaking strain for the float or hook and it will adversely influence the way the tackle performs. As a general guide, a light float requires a lightish line otherwise it won't cast very well and the line will drag it out of position. When you graduate into more specialist forms of fishing this particular rule can be broken but start out by making life easy for yourself!

Most newcomers mistakenly fish far too heavy, possibly with 4 to 6lb line, and wonder why they cannot hook a reasonable fish. The fact is that on many waters even a highly experienced angler would suffer the same lack of success using lines of that diameter.

For normal floatfishing requirements, reel lines of 2 to 3lb are satisfactory if matched with slightly lighter hooklengths. Today's advanced rods and reels are designed to cope with even finer lines without fear of breakages.

Fish are naturally inquisitive creatures but can become extremely wary, particularly on the more heavily fished waters. To overcome their natural caution you will need to fish delicate rigs.

Choosing the right float

When selecting a float, try running through the following questions:

- Will it carry sufficient shot to reach the spot where you want to cast the hookbait?

- On flowing waters, will it take enough weight down the line to get the hookbait down to the fish?

- Has the tip got the right amount of sensitivity or buoyancy for the conditions.

- Is the float long enough to combat surface drift? And is it short enough so as not to spook feeding fish in shallow water?

The floats on sale in your local tackle shop are attractive to the eye and most anglers hoard far more in their tackle box than they can ever possibly use. It's a fair bet you'll end up doing the same but at least try to satisfy practical demands if you can. Basically, there are three chief categories of float — sticks, wagglers and balsas.

Stick floats

These are designed exclusively for flowing water and are strapped to the line with two short lengths of silicone tubing fixed at the top and bottom of the float. There are three popular stick designs: the con-

ventional model with a wooden stem, modern plastic stem types and wire stems. Float manufacturers sometimes switch to plastics to find the right balance when suitably heavy wood is in short supply. We'll concentrate on the two main varieties, conventional wood stem and wire stem.

Wood stems

Most conventional sticks rely on a stem made from a heavy wood like lignum for their stability. This also aids casting and prevents the float from lifting out of the water excessively when the line is straightened to maintain tight control when trotting — letting the tackle travel in a controlled manner with the current. The action of straightening the line in this manner is known as **mending the line**.

Tips A heavier base material also helps to cock the float quickly. Clearly, you don't want the float to have travelled

halfway down the swim before it begins working correctly and registering bites. A balanced conventional stick is usually trotted through at the speed of the current. But it can be adapted for on-the-drop work, shallow or deep fishing and also slowed down, if you wish, to a complete stop.

● There is one very important point to grasp with all stick float fishing and that's the shotting method. The fewer shot you use to **dot down** a stick to its correct weighting, the less versatile it becomes. The essence of stick float work is that it is a method for searching out the fish in the swim. The idea is to juggle the shotting pattern to suit the changing whims of the fish as they rise in the water to feed in the upper layers or drop down to the bottom.

● Use a minimum of half-a-dozen

Mission accomplished on light float tackle and a big fish hits the net.

similar sized medium or small shot instead of two or three big ones. Then you'll have the flexibility to string out the shot when you feel you might get better results by presenting the hookbait on-the-drop. Or you can begin to bulk the the weights together when the fish congregate near the bottom. You could, of course, start off with two or three large bulk shot but you can't string them out sufficiently for a balanced, on-the-drop rig without completely taking the whole set-up to pieces which is time consuming.

Below: A very basic highly effective stick float shotting pattern. Start the session by trotting with the current using groups of bulk shot, later modify to a strung out (shirt button) on-the-drop rig. The change only takes a matter of seconds.

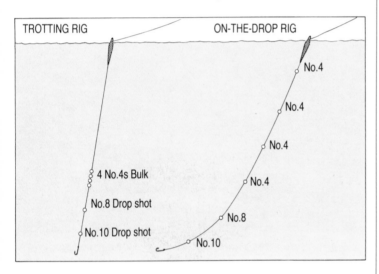

TROTTING RIG — ON-THE-DROP RIG

No.4
No.4
No.4
4 No.4s Bulk
No.4
No.8 Drop shot
No.8
No.10 Drop shot
No.10

Right top: Pointed and domed top sticks. The choice depends on the pace of the water.

Right: A brace of wire-stemmed sticks and traditional lignum patterns.

Wire Stems

The reason wire is used to replace a wooden stem is to give the float even greater stability, either in awkward blustery conditions or for faster, more turbulent currents.

The wire stem stick gives tighter control over the tackle thanks to the increased weight of the stem. This semi-cocks the float before the shotting has any effect. Wire stems are simple to fish and are recommended for novices. They're much easier to use on pacey rivers with a faster top layer of water. You can slow them down without flattening them out on the surface.

Tip shapes

The tips of stick float designs can vary from dome-shaped to gradually tapered or sharply pointed. These are not just cosmetic — they serve a purpose.

Domed top sticks are dotted down so they form just a dimple in the surface film. They work better on faster waters and are popular on powerful rivers like the Trent. Slightly tapered tips are more visible when the surface is choppy. Switch to a pointed tip when the fish become finicky as it presents less resistance to the bite. These types work best on slower moving waters for species like dace and roach.

Wagglers

The waggler family fall into three divisions — inserts, straights and bodied.

Insert wagglers

These sport a finer sight-tip for added sensitivity. They're the best float for taking quality fish on the far bank of canals and small rivers. And they are also superb stillwater floats, particularly for on-the-drop fishing.

Straight wagglers

These have no insert thus giving increased buoyancy at the tip making the float more visible in rough conditions. You can use the buoyant tip to its full advantage when fishing well overdepth on slow moving rivers, flowing canal venues and big lakes with strong surface drift. These floats can be anchored or at least slowed down on-the-trot, to present a hookbait more naturally when normal floats would shoot through the water too quickly.

Bodied wagglers

These take over when you are unable to cast the two previous designs the required distance because of high wind or other problems. The body gives extra weight carrying capacity and the longer stem helps to beat bad drift.

Because of their size, bodied floats are more stable in flowing water or drift. Under these conditions they'll slow down a hookbait's movement more effectively than a conventional waggler.

All wagglers are attached to the line by the base of the float and never with float rubbers or silicone tubing. Usually, a quick-change float adaptor is slipped over

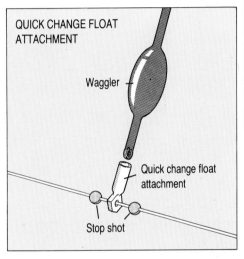

QUICK CHANGE FLOAT ATTACHMENT

Waggler

Quick change float attachment

Stop shot

Left: Bodied wagglers for fishing at distance.

Far left: Insert and straight wagglers.

the bottom eye. The base of the float simply plugs in the adaptor. That makes it easy to change the size of float without —having to break down the end tackle.

Wagglers are locked on the line with shot which should be evenly balanced on either side of the quick-change adaptor. For close-in work you can use small shot and bulk the main weight loading down the line. But for distance fishing very little weight is generally used down the rig. The majority is bulked around the float to assist effortless casting. Never try to even out the weight distribution between float and drop shot — you'll find the rig impossible to cast. At the very most, use only up to a third of a waggler's capacity down the line, the rest goes around the base of the float.

Balsas

There'll be a time when the stick float can't cope with the current, depth or distance you want to fish. This is when to switch to a larger float such as an Avon or all-balsa pattern.

The Avon

This is best described as a cross between a stick float and a balsa. It has a bulbous balsa body and stabilising cane or wire stem.

See-through Crystal wagglers are considered less visible to the fish. The beauty of this Drennan series is that the floats are take-apart and you can create your own patterns including the option to change tip colour.

BASIC BALSA RIG

Step up or down in shot
and float size to suit
conditions.

4 No.1s
Bulk shot

No.4 Dropper

Far Left: Balsa (left) and Chubber floats take over when the going gets too turbulent for the stick.

All balsas

There are two main designs of all-balsa floats: the conventional slimmer balsa tapers into a slight step at the sight tip for improved sensitivity; and the more awkward looking cigar-shaped balsas for carrying big baits in fast water, sometimes at long range.

These **Chubber type** floats, as they are known, are mainly meant for fishing with large pieces of breadflake, cubes of luncheon meat or lobworms. Their extra buoyancy and weighting capacity will cope with most of the rough water you're likely to come across. The normal all-balsa is really a scaled down version for use with smaller baits like casters and maggots. Conventional balsas work well in boiling slacks on flooded rivers and in areas where you can find a steadier pace on coloured, fast venues. Both designs respond best to bulk shotting and just one or two dropper shot.

Summing-up

Already you can see that each float design must be fished in a specific way and with the right shotting. There is a reason for more body or heavier stems and for different tip shapes.

The right rod

How do you define the right rod for floatfishing when there are so many lengths, actions and materials to consider?

Do you want a rod designed for a specialist form of floatfishing or will an all-rounder fit the bill? Frankly, what you settle for in the end all boils down to personal preference.

The material from which the rod blank is formed dictates the price tag. Fibreglass is cheap and if you are seeking a really low-cost entry into the sport then it's worth considering. But lightweight carbon is much more responsive and pleasing to handle. Prices in real terms have reduced over the years and there are now composite rods made from carbon and glass which represent good value for money.

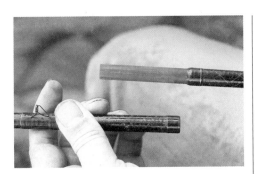

Spigot (right) or sleeve type (below) rod joints are equally efficient.

Actions and length

If you've got around £100 to spend you might find a rod made from a high modulous carbon or carbon and kevlar combination which will, in theory, meet all your floatfishing needs.

Lower down the price range a little more attention to rod action needs to be taken into account. Most anglers prefer a tip-actioned rod for stick float or balsa fishing, sometimes with a fine spliced tip if light lines are being used.

For waggler work, more of a through-action blank is used. This will punch out a float surprisingly well and with great accuracy.

Forget about test curves when choosing a float or match rod, the classification is in mere ounces, anyway. It is as well to go by feel when judging whether a rod is suitable for light line fishing.

The length of the rod is far more important. Don't make the mistake of selecting too short a rod because you will incur a loss of control over your tackle. Rods of 12 and 13ft will pick up the line on the strike far more effectively than 10 or 11ft models. As a guide, 12ft is a good length for canal fishing while 13ft is acceptable for most floatfishing needs including stick float and wagglers. Rods of 14ft or longer may have a control advantage when fishing the stick or any other top and bottom attached float but they become unwieldy for other forms of fishing.

There is a trend for the actual carbon content of a rod to be specified in percentages. It goes without saying that the rods with a higher percentage of carbon fibres cost more. But they are also thinner in diameter and much lighter. For example, a 12ft match rod can weigh as little as 4oz.

Top class float rods will deal with most, if not all, floatfishing demands. It is also at the top end where materials like boron and kevlar have been introduced to reinforce the performance qualities of these ultra-thin rods.

Boron tends to mellow a rod's action while kevlar tightens up on casting accuracy and the overall strength of a blank.

Far right: Rings with diamond-tough inserts improve the line flow on any float rod.

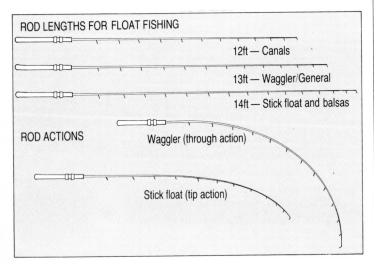

ROD LENGTHS FOR FLOAT FISHING

12ft — Canals

13ft — Waggler/General

14ft — Stick float and balsas

ROD ACTIONS

Waggler (through action)

Stick float (tip action)

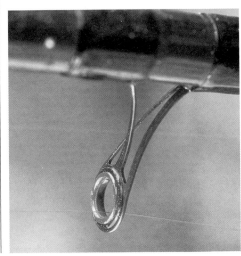

Ring types

Plain chrome rings are fitted to some float rods but you'll get more mileage out of those which have steel, ceramic or silicone carbide linings.

Chrome rings in their original blackened state are the most basic design and they remain surprisingly popular. The line runs through them sweetly enough but they soon start showing signs of wear and will need replacing regularly. With heavy use, chrome rings last about a year.

Lightweight ceramic or steel lined rings are fitted to nearly all the top rod designs and are very smooth running. Their life expectancy is several years.

The latest development is silicone carbide guides. These are very hard wearing and outlast all other designs but cost a small fortune. You will only find these installed on the most expensive rods.

Ring spacing varies on production rods although to be fair most manufacturers are now improving the relationship between the rings and the curve of the rod. If a good balance is found there will be few problems. But too few rings, particularly on the fine tip section, will cause the line to grate alarmingly when a big fish is being played.

A float rod should have a minimum of one intermediate ring every 30 centimetres (12in) of rod, although the rings are not spaced equal distances apart. They should gradually get closer together towards the tip.

Reel seats and handles

Reel fittings and cork handles used to be pretty standard but these days manufacturers are continually experimenting with new materials and designs. Chrome reel fittings seem to be on the way out but it's doubtful if cork handles will ever disappear. In the future there will be undoubtedly more rods with black duplon grips and other synthetic, waterproof handles.

As for reel seats on float rods, the most efficient newcomer is the moulded plastic John Roberts design which snugly holds the reel in place and is comfortable on the rod hand.

Some manufacturers make sure you position the reel correctly to achieve the right balance on the rod by restricting the manoeuvrability of sliding type collar fittings to the top of the handle. The number of anglers who insist on fishing with the reel down towards the butt clearly makes this a worthwhile innovation.

The right reel

Fixed spool reels are the leading models for floatfishing. They may be called open-faced because the line is visible when loaded compared with closed-face reels where it is hidden by the housing.

Open-faced reels are very versatile. They're ideal for all waggler fishing, especially long range work, as an ultra shallow

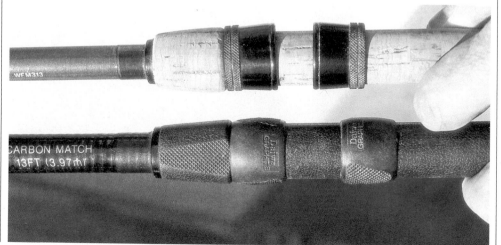

The comfort of a cork handle (top) still takes some beating. But there has been a move towards synthetics which look and feel much like the material from which car steering wheels are manufactured.

spool will prevent the line from bedding down and fouling itself during repeated casting and retrieving.

These reels are also suitable for stick and balsa fishing but their downfall comes in a facing wind when the line will tend to blow back over the bale arm. That's when many anglers switch to a closed face model with its internal line spool which is shielded from wind.

Before buying a fixed spool, check that your forefinger can comfortably touch the forward lip of the line spool when the reel is fixed in place on the rod. You'll need to feather line off the reel with this finger of your rod hand while trotting with an open bale arm.

Then confirm that the bale arm closes smoothly when engaged by winding the handle. If it causes a severe jolt then you're likely to lose fish when trotting a float. Ideally, the bale takes the line smoothly off your forefinger after the strike has been made and a fish hooked.

Many fixed spool reels are sold with an ultra shallow spool that is perfectly loaded when 100 metres of 2-3lb line are wound on. That compares with a deep spool which might swallow at least 300 metres of the same breaking strain. Apart from being more expensive to load, deep spools

Top: The clean lines of a Browning fixed-spool reel.

Above: Deep spool (left) for heavier lines and match spool.

Right: The spool must be within easy reach of the forefinger for efficient one-handed control.

tend to cause line bedding.

If your reel offers the option of deep or shallow spools it will widen its scope at a later stage when you might want to store 4 or 6lb line on a spare spool for legering.

Clutch, bale and roller

Clutch or drag systems can be pre-set at varying degrees of tension to allow the spool to rotate and release line with the bale arm closed. This is a useful safeguard with light line as the drag can be finely adjusted to give line to a big fish before its powerful boring exerts more pressure than the breaking strain of the nylon can withstand.

It is also a useful cushion if you strike too hard with the anti-reverse on. This is the switch which stops the handle rotating backwards and means you can strike one-handed.

Clutch mechanisms are now largely installed at the rear of the reel where they are much easier to operate should adjustment prove necessary during the playing of a fish. They have become known as sterndrags.

The automatic bale arm speeds up casting and your fishing technique as a whole. It is only available at the top end of the reel market on models like the Mitchell Match 440A, Daiwa Autocast and the Ryobi Mastermatch. All these reels allow the bale arm to be opened with the forefinger of the rod hand by depressing the bale or operating a trigger mechanism.

Left: A bale arm roller. This mechanism combats line wear.

Below: A sterndrag with positive graduated settings.

Left: Three top class reels fitted with automatic bale arms.

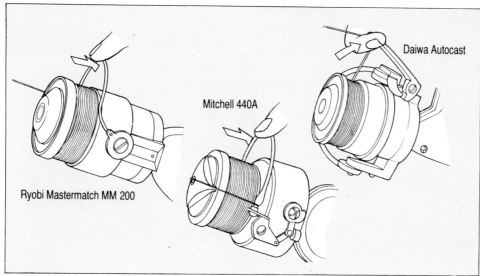

Ryobi Mastermatch MM 200

Mitchell 440A

Daiwa Autocast

With normal reels you have to open the bale arm with your free hand first before trapping the line against the spool with the rod hand.

The rate at which reels retrieve line back onto the spool varies between models but this isn't critical.

Finally, purchase a reel which incorporates an efficient line roller on the bale arm. This will virtually eliminate line grooving. The majority of reels possess a roller but if yours doesn't then keep an eye open for signs of wear as a groove on the bale arm will rapidly damage the line.

Closed-face confusion

There's considerable confusion in coarse fishing about the role of the **closed-face** reel. The reason for this probably arises because some top anglers seem content using this reel for tasks that seem beyond its scope in the hands of the average angler.

Generally, closed-face reels are a safe bet for stick float fishing and certain forms of waggler use. They're popular for trotting sticks because of the superb control

Right: Closed-face helps keep wind tangles at bay.

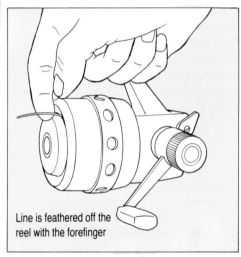

Line is feathered off the reel with the forefinger

When to use closed-face reels with float gear. Because a facing wind can defeat more accurate open-faced reels (when fishing tight in to the bank) it may be advisable to switch to a closed-face model. This eliminates the possibility of bad tangles if the line blows back over the bale arm on the open-faced model. The difference needed to bring back a degree of accuracy would be a slightly larger float, with an additional BB weight loading.

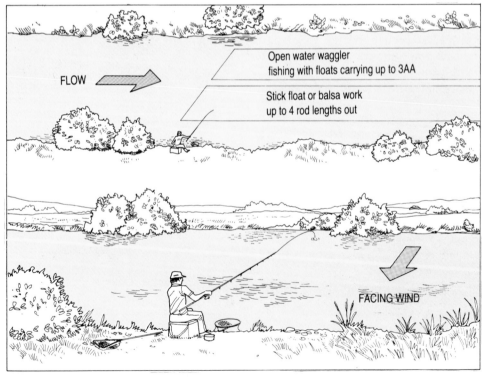

FLOW

Open water waggler fishing with floats carrying up to 3AA

Stick float or balsa work up to 4 rod lengths out

FACING WIND

they give in feeding line at differing rates to let a float push through naturally or to hold it back against the flow. Better still is the smooth pick-up when a fish has been hooked. This compares very favourably with the nasty kick you tend to get with some open-faced reels when the bale arm is engaged following the strike. This sudden jolt can result in fish being bumped off the hook.

As line feeds off the spool from within the housing on the closed-face, there is a certain amount of friction although not sufficient to damage the nylon in any way. But it's enough to restrict the flow of the cast and that's a drawback when trying to achieve spot-on accuracy with the waggler. It would certainly make it difficult to consistently place a waggler within inches of far bank cover.

Open-faced reels are preferred for the bulk of waggler fishing but the closed-face is called up when a facing wind blows line back over the bale arm producing frustrating tangles. If you're forced to switch reels for this reason during a session then change to a slightly heavier float to achieve the same casting distance with the closed-face.

A final point on closed-face reels concerns the line loading. This shouldn't be a problem with the latest designs which have wider spools and will easily hold in excess of 100 metres of 2 to 3lb line. But if you find yourself with a narrow, deepish spool don't try backing it out with spare nylon to bring up the level — the reel line will bed in badly. Instead, load the spool with the minimum of line — 40 to 50 metres — then line flow will not prove a problem.

The right line

You can buy spools of frail nylon with a breaking strain calculated in ounces right through to the heavyweight sea lines offering complete security up to 100lb and more. The different brands also vary in colour which isn't important for reel lines but can affect hooklengths.

Some special hooklength lines are sold in 50 metre spools but usually lines are packaged in 100 metre lengths. Providing you have a shallow spool on your reel, this is more than adequate for floatfishing.

A trend you'll have to monitor when choosing modern line is the swing towards low diameter monofilaments. These claim the same breaking strain as standard lines but with a greatly reduced diameter. Obviously, this is a good idea in theory because thinner lines cast better and bring you more bites when used as hooklengths.

But to achieve such a low diameter, the line is pre-stretched and this eliminates a great deal of its ability to absorb shock impact. For the novice, indeed even expert anglers, this loss of elasticity can be disastrous because a hasty strike can result in break-offs — losing a lot of tackle and perhaps leaving a hook in a fish.

A good many experienced anglers are wary of adapting to this new technology. The new line may break at its stated breaking strain under gradually applied tension but during fishing, things rarely happen that way. If in doubt, leave the low diameter lines alone until you've gained the necessary experience to feel confident about experimenting further.

Standard lines will catch you plenty of fish anyway. The differences in diameter on light hooklengths are so minimal that good tackle presentation can overcome the slight increase in thickness compared with a pre-stretched nylon.

Colour factors

Lines are dyed numerous shades from black to green. On the reel, none of this matters very much but with hooklengths a little care should be taken. For instance, in bright sunny conditions on a gin-clear water it is inadvisable to use a black dyed line because it will stand out like a sore thumb.

But the same line would probably work very well in coloured, muddy water. If the hooklength is being fished overdepth, a black line on a dark, muddy bottom will blend in well.

It's all a matter of simple logic. Just remember to use clear lines for on-the-drop fishing and dark lines for bottom fishing

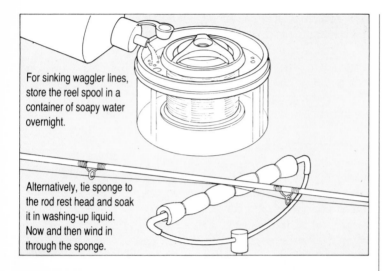

For sinking waggler lines, store the reel spool in a container of soapy water overnight.

Alternatively, tie sponge to the rod rest head and soak it in washing-up liquid. Now and then wind in through the sponge.

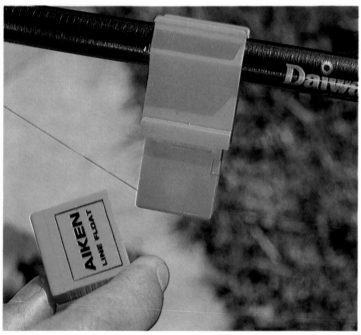

A fast way to make your line stay up top. This Aiken product contains specially treated pads through which the line is retrieved to smear it with floatant.

Sinkers and floaters

Unfortunately, line manufacturers don't seem too keen on describing their lines as sinkers or floaters. They leave it up to the angler to find out for himself.

Daiwa Harrier, Drennan Floatfish and standard Bayer Perlon are all good floating lines. Maxima, Racine and Drennan Specimen are excellent sinkers. There are plenty of other makes, too, if you wish to experiment. As a guide, shiny lines float well and matt finished lines sink.

Sometimes new lines will not behave correctly until they have been broken in. This particularly applies to sinking lines which are best soaked in a container of soapy water, preferably the night before a trip.

Another dodge is to strap a strip of sponge soaked in washing up liquid around the rod-rest head. The line is wound in through the sponge from time to time to keep it smeared with detergent.

As for floating lines, you can reel them in occasionally through a pad of **floatant grease** which is marketed in tins for fly-fishing or spray them with a Leeda aerosol intended for dry flies.

Better still, Aiken offer a clever device that snaps on the rod just above the reel. The line is clipped between two pads of floatant and as you wind in the line is treated very quickly and effectively.

We'll be looking again at hooklength lines in more detail for river and lake fishing, but it is worth carrying a selection ranging from 1lb breaking strain for when the fishing is hard, through to 1.5 or 1.7lb for normal conditions and 2 or 2.5lb in case big fish are expected on the float.

The right hook

The most widely used hooks are spade-ends which have a flattened top to the shank. The line is knotted on the shank and prevented from slipping off the hook by the spade-like, flattened shape.

Eyed hooks are formed by bending the top of the shank into a small circle through which the line is threaded and tied on the shank or directly knotted to the eye itself.

and you won't go far wrong.

As for breaking strains, try and use the lightest you feel happy with because the thinner diameter does make tackle presentation and casting a lot easier. There is no need to go below 2lb — very fine lines wear much too quickly on the reel and can let you down badly at critical moments of stress.

The average angler will more than likely carry a spool of 2.5 or 3lb sinking line for most of his waggler fishing and another spool of the same breaking strain but in a floating line for stick or balsa work. Most matchmen, however, tend to step down to 2lb in both cases.

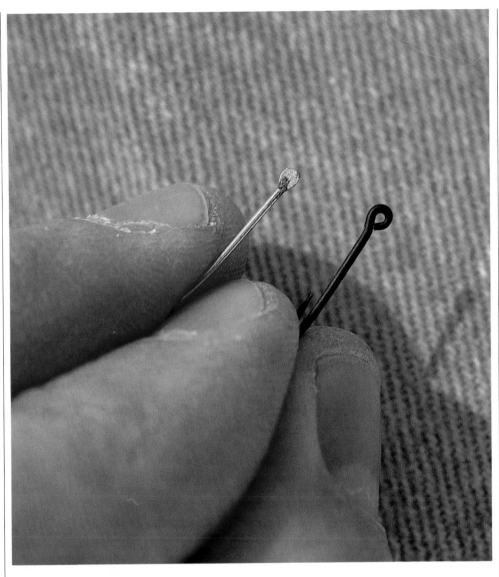

Spade-end patterns are more tricky to tie than eyed hooks but it's worth the effort because they give superior presentation, particularly with small hooks.

If you're all fingers and thumbs, then try one of the commercial hook tiers. The Matchman and Specialist Hook Tiers are among the best. The Matchman ties spades while the Specialist will deal with eyed hooks as well.

As a last resort, ready-tied hooks are available but they're expensive.

How they are numbered

The standard numbering of hook sizes in this country for freshwater use starts at 2, which is the largest, and runs in even numbers up to a tiny 26. On the Conti-nent, odd numbered hooks are also used and some of these have found their way into specialist tackle shops in Britain.

Bigger hooks between 2 and 8 are intended for big baits like luncheon meat, lumps of bread and boilies.

Middle-range hooks from size 10 to 16 can be used with the same baits scaled down in size plus sweetcorn, worms and groupings of smaller offerings like maggots and casters. Small hooks from 18 down are for baits like maggot, caster, hemp, tare, breadpunch and bloodworm.

Size considerations

Selecting a suitable hook size must take into account the type of bait being used and target species. The swim you're

Spade or eyed? It's worth taking the trouble to perfect the spade-end hook tying — the end product gives superior presentation.

fishing could affect the eventual choice as well.

In theory, you want the hook size to perfectly match the bait. The hook needs to be as small and unobtrusive as possible with small baits and as big as you can get away with for better penetration using larger baits.

Shy biting fish like dace and roach will often give unhittable bites if the hook size is too large. They can see the hook so they simply pluck at the bait without taking it down. In this case try and find a hook you can completely hide in a bait like casters — an 18 would be suitable— or scale down to a 20 with offerings like maggots where the hook point must be left exposed for efficient penentration. You'll also find hook size important on gin clear or hard fished waters. Where you might tempt bites on a size 14 or 16 with maggot on an easy water, a hard venue is more likely to need 18 or 20 hooks for a response.

Another important hook factor is the shape of the pattern you choose and the thickness of the wire.

The most popular freshwater hook patterns are the crystal bend and the round bend. Both are obtainable in a range of wire gauges. Obviously, finer wire is used with smaller, lighter baits so as to give them a more natural fall through the water. If big fish are expected you may have to settle for a thicker, forged hook regardless. Hook shape is normally determined by the bait. Maggots and worms tend to stay on a crystal bend better whereas on a round bend they can fly off on the cast. Casters suit either design but seed baits like hemp, tares and sweetcorn are more effective on round bends as their wider gape gives improved hooking with these harder skinned baits.

Barbed or barbless?

Some fisheries have banned barbed hooks. This can cause problems as maggots, for example, can fall off barbless hooks on the cast although baits like bread and corn are unaffected.

The solution is to flatten the barb on a barbed hook leaving a slight bump which will keep the bait in place. To all intents and purposes you are now fishing with a

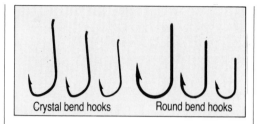

Crystal bend hooks   Round bend hooks

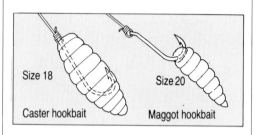

Size 18

Caster hookbait

Size 20

Maggot hookbait

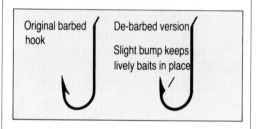

Original barbed hook

De-barbed version

Slight bump keeps lively baits in place

barbless pattern and obeying the rules of the fishery.

In fact, if you can use barbless hooks they are much kinder on the fish and penetrate more effectively on the strike. You will not lose more fish on them — the only time a barbless design is likely to come adrift is if you give a fish slack line. And that should be avoided with any type of hook.

Putting it all together

Once you've sorted out all your tackle for a floatfishing session, assembly is straightforward. First, the line is loaded on the reel and to avoid twist it should be wound on in the same direction it leaves the manufacturer's plastic spool.

Fill the reel until the line level is just below the lip of the spool and then it will peel off smoothly. Never underfill a spool otherwise the line will scrape against the lip causing friction and retarding its flow.

When the reel has been fitted to the rod at the top of the handle, open the bale-arm and thread the line through the rod

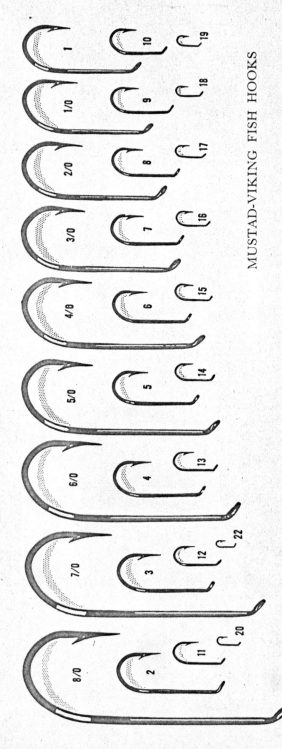

MUSTAD-VIKING FISH HOOKS

The illustration at the left indicates and names the various parts of a fish hook and makes clear two important dimensions viz: the gap and the throat of the hook. The hook shown is of Mustad-Viking pattern. Note the width of the gap, the clearance between the point and the shank of the hook. Note also the depth of the throat of the hook. These generous dimensions provide for a more generous bite, deeper penetration of point and better holding power. The weight of the fish is carried well up on the centre of the bend.

The size of a fish hook depends upon the pattern of the hook and is indicated by the width of the gap of the hook. For example: the illustration above pictures Mustad-Viking fish hooks Quality No. 7958. Each hook is shown in its true size and size number and all hooks of Mustad-Viking pattern conform to these sizes.

The hook sizes of other patterns will differ to some extent therefore when speaking or writing about fish hooks the quality number and the size number of the hook should be kept inseparable.

rings making sure they have been lined up in a perfectly straight line on each section of the rod. If it's windy, point the rod away from the direction of the gusts to prevent the line blowing back over the reel's bale-arm and tangling.

Once the line has been fed through all the rings, pull several feet off the reel and you can put the rod down in its rests while the end tackle is sorted out. The float goes on first, either as a double-rubber if it's a top and bottom model or locked by shot if you're fishing the waggler.

Position the float a couple of feet away from the end of the line so it doesn't impede tying on the hooklength. There are two good line to line knots for attaching hooklengths — the loop to loop and blood knot.

When the hooklength is attached it is better to shot-up the rig correctly at this stage placing any bulk shot above the joining knot and the tell-tale droppers on the hooklength. Make sure the hooklength is not too short, 45 centimetres (18in) is about right to retain some of the stretch of this lighter line.

After you've checked the float is cocking satisfactorily, the final job is to tie on the hook. There are many hook knots, those shown are the easiest and most secure.

All that remains is to plumb up the depth and space the tackle out accordingly. We'll be looking at this in the next chapter.

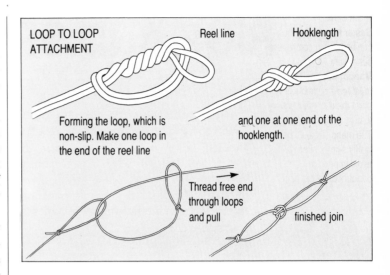

Top: Loop to loop attachment. The most popular way of attaching a hooklength to the reel line.

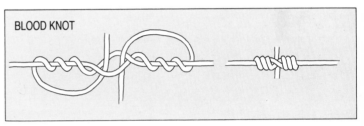

Above: Blood knot. An alternative method of securing the hooklength to the reel line. his knot is often preferred by match anglers.

Below: A. How to tie an eyed-hook knot formed above the hook. **B.** How to tie an eyed-hook with knot formed on the shank. **C.** Conventional spade-end knot. It takes pratise to tie this knot without damaging the line. **D.** Reversed spade-end knot. A foolproof knot which will not damage the line because the knot is tightened by pulling the loose end.

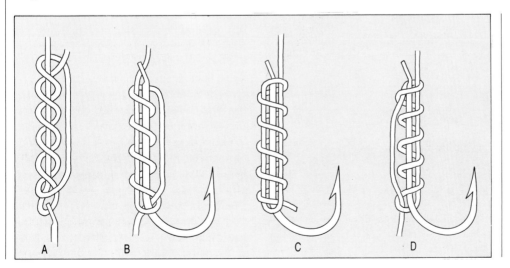

RIGS AND SPECIALS

Anybody can strap the first float that comes to hand on the line and string a few shot out below until it sits neatly in the water. But you will only achieve consistently good results in coarse fishing if you understand the tactical thinking behind float selection and shotting arrangements.

How to position the silicone on a double-rubber float.

Knowing what you are setting out to achieve gives a basis for meaningful experiment. Frequently, it's minor adjustments of shotting that turn a moderately successful rig into a real winner on the day.

The starting point in float selection is the type of venue being fished. This largely dictates the pattern of float you use and shotting required. Float attachment falls into the two basic categories:

Double-rubber — attached to the line at top and bottom.

Bottom-end only — attached, naturally enough at the bottom only.

Understanding which to use is the beginning of the decision-making process which leads to expertise in shotting.

Double-rubber or bottom ender?

Double-rubbers, are nearly always fished on flowing water where they give more control than bottom-enders. That is not to say that bottom-end floats are ruled out — they can be just as good if the fish will only bite when the hookbait is presented in a specific way. But remember they are less versatile and consistent on running water.

The reverse applies on stillwaters where bottom-end floats come into their own because they are more stable. That's particularly the case when the line from rod tip to float is submerged beneath the surface. A double-ended float will not work this way since the line has to remain on the surface for a clean strike to be made. Without a current to work against, double-ended floats become very unstable. Wind or surface drift quickly puts them off course.

With a bottom-ender, the only modification you have to make, assuming the line has been sunk to defeat drifting, is to strike sideways instead of upwards in order to set the hook home.

The only time a top and bottom float has an application on stillwaters is when fishing the margins with the float directly under the rod tip, or when the tackle is dropped into a hole among very thick weed where it will be prevented from drifting.

Remember we are talking about **running line rigs** here. Later you will discover that top and bottom attached floats can be used to very good effect when pole fishing on stillwaters where the control over the tackle is that much greater.

Shot position

The biggest difference between river and lake rigs, apart from the float, is the position of the shot. On flowing water more weight tends to be used down the line to keep the hookbait near, or on, the bottom. But a leisurely fall of the hookbait can be beneficial on stillwaters where rigs tend to be fished further out and the main shot loading is around the float.

River rigs and how to use them

Stick floats

The stick float is the most popular design for river fishing and as discussed on page 48 you'll come across several types in the shops. Traditionally, sticks have been made with a heavy wooden base for stability but a lighter base performs well when fishing on-the-drop for species like dace and chub because it slows the way the rig settles.

A good example of a modern plastic-stemmed stick is the Drennan Grey with its see-through base. This is suited to clear, shallow swims on rivers where in bright light it will not cast such a big shadow over the bottom as it travels downstream.

Conventional wire stem and lignum based sticks will partly cock in the water before the shotting comes into play and should cover most of your stick float fishing in deeper, faster swims.

Sluggish water

Let's assume you want to fish a sluggish river using the on-the-drop style. Select a

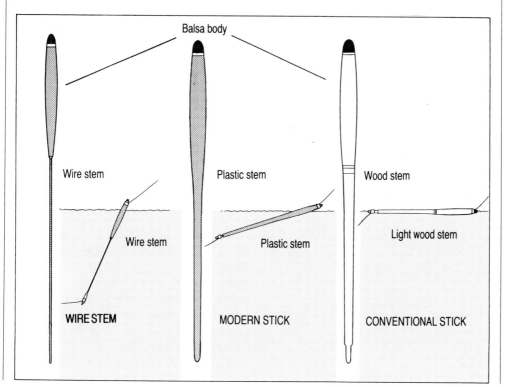

Balsa body

Wire stem

Wire stem

WIRE STEM

Plastic stem

Plastic stem

MODERN STICK

Wood stem

Light wood stem

CONVENTIONAL STICK

Stick floats and how they behave on landing.

stick with a light wooden stem to carry just over six No.6 shot. Space out four of the shot at equal distances between the float and hooklength, storing the remaining two directly underneath the float. For the time being, these two shot will balance the light float, making it react in much the same way as a heavy based stick.

The rig is completed by adding a No.8 about a third of the way down the hooklength and a No.10 micro-shot between this and the hook. Now the rig is nicely balanced to allow you to search out the swim with plenty of shot spread down the line which can be shuffled around if need be to change the way the hookbait behaves.

With the shot spread out, the float can be held on a tight line as it hits the water and the tackle will fall at a slower rate of descent for on-the-drop bites. Or you can let the float run the second it hits the water and the hookbait and shot will settle a lot quicker.

It's also possible to fish this set-up overdepth by **deepening-off** (lengthening the line between float and hook) by a foot or two and holding back hard on the float.

The great thing about this rig is its flexibility. If the fish stay deep in the water some or all the No.6 shot are moved down to a point just above the hooklength to form a bulk shotting pattern. This will considerably speed up the fall of the hookbait.

When the fish rise in the water, the two No.6s originally stored under the float are spread out in unison with the other four split-shot to slow the rate at which the float and tackle settles through the water. Often, this ploy brings very savage takes on-the-drop.

Medium-paced water

A plastic or heavier wooden-stemmed stick float is likely to be selected on medium-paced water. The objectives are much the same as with the lighter, wooden-based float. All that changes is the shotting which would normally be slightly heavier — possibly substituting the No.6s with No.4s.

The reason for upping the weight loading is to stabilise the rig against the stronger current otherwise the float would lift up flat on the surface, when held back, or scoot through the swim too fast. The increased loading obviously means a bigger float must also be used.

The starting point for this rig is to evenly space out between four and eight No.4s down to the hooklength.

As a guide, you'll require one No.4 for each foot of water fished, excluding the hooklength. If the hooklength is the standard 54cm (18in), it takes a No.6 followed by a No.8 dust-shot fixed 15 to 30cm (six or eight inches) from the hook.

Faster water

For faster water where the surface of the river is possibly even boiling slightly, the wire stem stick is very useful. Its extra stem weighting also makes life easier when wind causes presentation problems. Oddly, the same kind of shotting as conventional sticks usually does the trick. The float switch itself is sufficient to restablish control on the faster flow rate.

The sign that the stick float has reached

**Light stick rigs.
Below left**: This set-up is the starting point and can satisfy a variety of syles — including on-the-drop and dragging overdepth.
Below right: When fish are feeding near the bottom the rig is modified to bulk shotting.

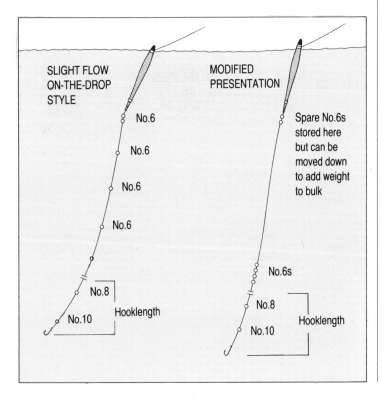

SLIGHT FLOW ON-THE-DROP STYLE

No.6

No.6

No.6

No.6

No.8

No.10

Hooklength

MODIFIED PRESENTATION

Spare No.6s stored here but can be moved down to add weight to bulk

No.6s

No.8

No.10

Hooklength

its limits of use is when it cannot be held back against the current without riding up too high or flattening out completely on the surface. Another indication that the stick is running through too quickly for a fish to intercept the hookbait is when the float tip leans away from you as it procedes down the swim.

Providing you've fixed the stick or any other kind of top and bottom float correctly on the line with silicone tubing, it should always lean back slightly towards you as it trots down the swim. If it's upright or leaning away then you're not controlling it properly or the tackle is out of balance.

With lighter stick floats there are a couple of tricks worth trying if the float fails to behave properly because of the conditions. In fast currents, you can overshot the rig so it must be fished on a tight line to keep the float tip visible. Overshot by one, two or three No.4s while attempting this tactic to slow the tackle down.

The other dodge is to **backshot** in awkward downstream winds to try and prevent the line overtaking the float or bowing out and pulling it off course. Depending on the strength of the wind, fix a shot between a No.8 and 4 approximately 30

to 60 cm (one to two feet) above the float to help control the line and keep it directly behind the float.

Balsas and Avons

There'll be times when the stick float can't cope with the current, depth or distance you want to fish. That's the moment to call up an Avon or all-balsa design.

All-Balsas

The conventional all-balsa model has a streamlined body which tapers into a slight step at the sight tip for better sensitivity. The other all-balsa design called the Chubber is cigar-shaped and its role is to carry big baits through fast water, sometimes at long range. It's buoyant at the tip and will take weighty baits like large chunks of breadflake, cubes of luncheon meat or lobworms. The streamlined balsa is really a scaled down version for use with smaller baits like casters and maggots. It's also a good choice for tackling boily (see page 63) swims on a flooded river.

Both these balsa floats need to be bulk

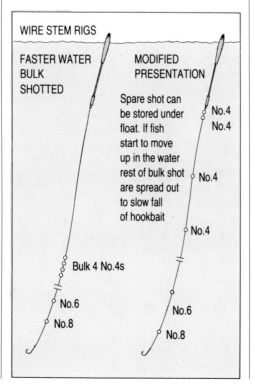

MEDIUM FLOW ON-THE-DROP STYLE

No.4

No.4

No.4

No.4

Bulk the No.4s shown for fishing a bait close to or on the bottom

No.4s

No.6

No.8

No.6

No.8

WIRE STEM RIGS

FASTER WATER BULK SHOTTED

MODIFIED PRESENTATION

Spare shot can be stored under float. If fish start to move up in the water rest of bulk shot are spread out to slow fall of hookbait

No.4

No.4

No.4

No.4

Bulk 4 No.4s

No.6

No.8

No.6

No.8

Conventional stick rigs.
Left: (left) This example is recommended for a swim of about 1.2m (4ft) in depth. Add an extra No.4 per extra 25cm (foot) of water and increase the float size to accomodate.

Right: Wire stem rigs.

shotted with just one or two dropper shot. They are not suitable for on-the-drop fishing and are certainly less versatile than the stick float.

Avons

Among the jobs for the Avon float is long-trotting on streamy runs where fish like big roach and chub are expected. The slightly prouder sight tip on this float shows up well at long range. Again, bulk shotting with one or two dropper-shot is recommended. It can also carry longer strings of scaled down bulk shot to pick up undertow in deep swims.

A traditional technique is to fish the Avon with a free-running centrepin reel which helps slow the hookbait to a more natural speed.

Neat side-eye on a balsa slider

Below right: Shotting close-range rigs.

Below left:
A. Conventional balsa.
B. Chubber type balsa.
C. Conventional Avon.
D. Wire-stem Avon.

Lake rigs

Close-range lake rigs

Several float designs cope equally well with canal or lake fishing although their size is a limiting factor, as far as distance casting is concerned, on the bigger expanses of water.

For close range lake fishing the Drennan Canal Crystal is excellent in shallow, clear swims. This see-through float doesn't throw a shadow on the bottom and has a

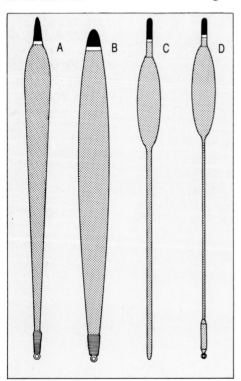

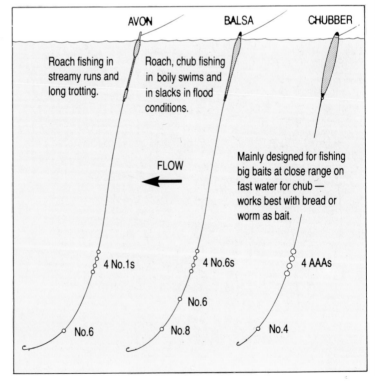

AVON — Roach fishing in streamy runs and long trotting.

BALSA — Roach, chub fishing in boily swims and in slacks in flood conditions.

CHUBBER — Mainly designed for fishing big baits at close range on fast water for chub — works best with bread or worm as bait.

FLOW

4 No.1s — No.6

4 No.6s — No.6 — No.8

4 AAAs — No.4

very sensitive tip. It performs most effectively carrying up to 3BB locking-shot and a couple of lightish dropper-shot for fishing on-the-drop style or on the bottom. It's a float to use with light line and small baits for small fish.

Sarkandas waggler

A slightly different version of this float is the Sarkandas waggler with an extra long, fine nylon sight-tip. It's locked on the line the same way with up to 3BB or 2AA shot. The main application is for fish like skimmer bream and tench which often give tiny indications on a float without actually taking the hookbait positively. If you use a longer, finer tip these bites show up better and you can wait until the float sinks away properly.

To achieve an even more positive indication, fish with an extra No.6 or 4 shot on the bottom positioned several inches below the hookbait. When a fish picks up the bait, the extra weight sinks the float very decisively.

Stillwater Blue

When surface drift makes the Canal Crystal or extra long Insert Sarkandas lose stability, then the Stillwater Blue is a better bet. Its lower slung body and slightly increased weight carrying capacity gives it better holding power in drift. It is fished with similar shotting patterns — perhaps with just a little more weight around the float and an extra No.8 or so down the rig.

Middle distance and long range

Most middle distance and long range stillwater floatfishing revolves around Insert, straight and bodied wagglers.

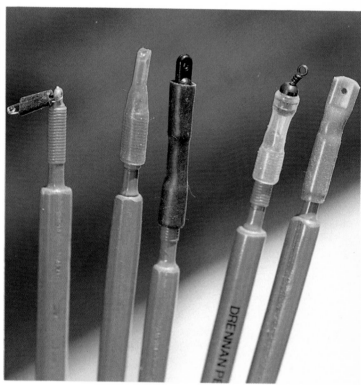

Below: Quick-change float adaptors make life a lot easier when you're forced to permutate rigs.

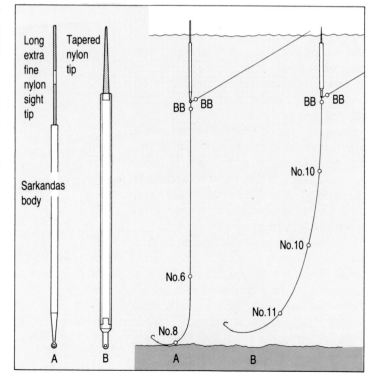

A. Extra-fine insert waggler. A good laying-on float. The extra-long tip shows lift bites well. Add an extra No.6 or No.4 at No.8 position for more positive bites when fishing over depth

B. Drennan Canal Crystal. An on-the-drop rig for clean shallow lakes.

Right: Shotting for the Stillwater Blue.

Far right: Wimet Safeweights are fine as locking-shot with a light waggler. Unlike many of the larger shot sizes in other brands, they're kind on nylon and no silicone buffer is required.

Opposite left: Rig for fishing tight into cover or shallow water up to 1.2m in depth (left). A slightly bigger insert waggler for deeper water — more shot is added down the line (right).

Opposite middle: A shallow water rig (left) that takes over when the insert float is difficult to see or is dragged under by drift. A deeper straight waggler rig (right). If a single No.8 drag shot fails to steady the rig, try trimming a little weight from the locking shot and putting another No.8 or two down the line, 2.5cm apart, on the hooklength.

Opposite right: Shotting can be modified for on-the-drop fishing but fish slightly heavier for more positive registration i.e. string out several No.8 shot.

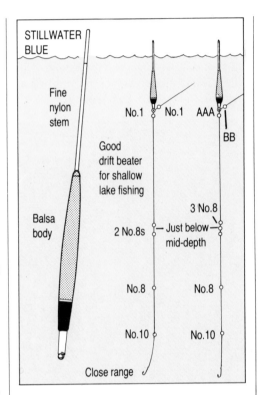

STILLWATER BLUE

Fine nylon stem

Balsa body

No.1 No.1 AAA BB

Good drift beater for shallow lake fishing

3 No.8
2 No.8s — Just below — mid-depth

No.8 No.8

No.10 No.10

Close range

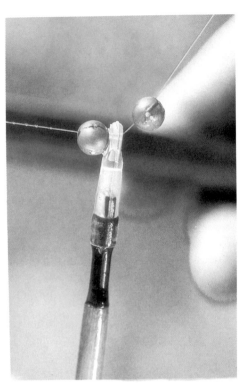

Insert wagglers

These were described on page 32 as being the best float for fishing the far bank of small rivers and canals. This is because they cast very accurately to fishy-looking cover often found on the far side of these waterways.

The same situation arises on lakes when the fish are lying against rushes on the far side of narrow bays or beneath foliage overhanging from islands. But the insert waggler has a great deal to offer apart from casting accuracy. It will carry plenty of weight for casting out fair distances and still remain sensitive by virtue of its fine tip. Inserts made from fine plastic, nylon or Sarkandas will sink away under a mere No.8 or 10 shot. Therefore, it's unlikely that fish will feel much resistance when towing them under.

Lake fish have plenty of time to reject a suspicious offering but the insert gives similar sensitivity to a much smaller float at a greatly increased distance. It usually brings very positive bites. As with most waggler rigs, inserts work best with the bulk weighting around the float base. Non-toxic shot like the Wimet Safeweights which team well with lighter

wagglers may begin to slip if used as locking-shot because of the much greater strain imposed. The solution is to secure them with No.8 lead shot.

Shotting down the line is determined by the type of swim being fished. If the float needs to be cast tight to far bank or island cover, then very light shot is fixed down the line so it doesn't influence the way the float flies through the air. In shallow water or for mid-depth fishing, two No.8s or 10s or a mixture is usually enough.

In deeper, open water a few more shot may be positioned below the float to stabilise the rig. Several No.8s spread out in stick float fashion is OK. Otherwise, step up to something like a No.4 or 5 just below mid-depth and taper the drop-shot down to a No.7 or 8, then a 10.

Straight wagglers

These take over from the insert design if drift pulls the finer tipped float under when the hookbait is presented on the bottom — or choppy conditions make it difficult to see the insert. Several small shot can be dragged around on the bottom by a straight waggler if required to try and anchor the rig.

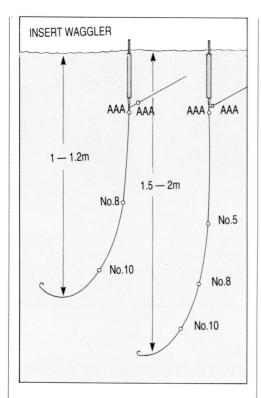

INSERT WAGGLER

AAA AAA   AAA AAA

1 — 1.2m

1.5 — 2m

No.8

No.5

No.10

No.8

No.10

STRAIGHT WAGGLER

AAA
AAA   AAA AAA

1 — 1.2m   2 — 2.5m

DRIFT

No.4   No.4

No.6

No.6

No.8 (drag shot)   Drag shot (2 or 3 No. 8s)

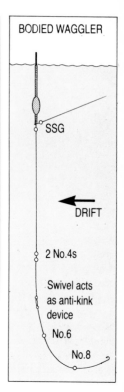

BODIED WAGGLER

SSG

DRIFT

2 No.4s

Swivel acts
as anti-kink
device

No.6

No.8

Straights are bulk-shotted much the same as Inserts but leave just a little bit more weight loading to go down the line.

Insert or straight wagglers will comfortably cope with distances up to five or six rod lengths in normal conditions. Beyond that range, or when wind or drift make fishing even shorter distances a struggle, then change to a big bodied waggler.

Commercial models take up to three or four swan shot but many anglers construct specials taking a lot more than that—some even Araldite an Arlesey bomb in the base! These hefty missiles are built for reaching bream or carp at very long range on shallow, clear lakes.

Bodied wagglers

These are usually fished from five to eight rod lengths out and because big, robust shot are needed to lock them on the line it's recommended that you use hard, non-toxic brands like Thamesly Sure Shot. Remember to close them on a silicone buffer to avoid damaging the line.

Again, when stepping up in float size a little more shot is needed down the line to balance the rig. Two or three No.4 shot fixed a little below half-depth are ade-quate, tapering off with a No.6 followed by an 8. It's possible that you'll find the hooklength twisting on the retrieve with these big floats. This tends to happen particularly when using double caster or maggot which set up a spinning action when reeled in quickly. The answer is to join the hooklength to the main line with a swivel which acts as an anti-kink device.

Apart from being very effective on lakes, bodied wagglers can be used on flowing

If you want to use Wimet weights as lockers with a heavy waggler, then you'll need to prevent them slipping along the line. One solution is to secure them in position with No.8 lead shot which are not outlawed.

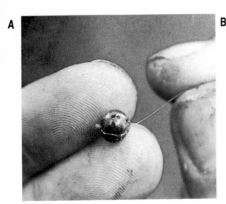
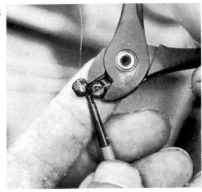
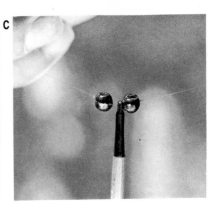

Above:
Fixing a silicone buffer
A. Most large sizes of shot need a silicone buffer when used as lockers on a waggler. Cut a length of silicone to the full width of the shot and gently fix on the line as shown.
B. Once positioned, trap the lockers securely with shot-pliers.
C. Leave some room for movement between the shot so the waggler can collapse with less splash on entering the water.

Above right: Choose between a tiny eye or swivel on a bottom-end only slider.

water. When it is not feasible to fish a top and bottom float they are the next best thing to slow a hookbait down with their extra weight. A two swan bodied waggler will trot through a lot slower than a 2AAA or 3AAA straight or insert waggler.

Special floats

Canal Greys

The Canal Grey float was developed by matchman Billy Makin and has become a classic. It is a brilliant, all-purpose bottom-ender made from balsa, and tapering to a very fine tip. It works very differently to the normal peacock and sarkandas wagglers. Stability and super sensitivity are its strengths and it comes into its own in the 2 to 3BB sizes for fishing two thirds of the way across canals with baits like breadpunch, squatts and pinkies on running line. (See page 56.)

The Canal Grey is weighted like a waggler with bulk locking-shot and very small drop-shot, normally No.10s or 11s (right). It can be fished on-the-drop or dragging over-depth. Its streamlined shape casts well but it is quite a dumpy float and will not spook fish in shallow, clear water.

Compared with an insert waggler, the Canal Grey has a gradual taper to the fine tip which signals on-the-drop bites very well indeed. It is so sensitive that some pole anglers use the float, shotted lightly with small-lockers and Olivettes as bulk 50cm (18in) or so from the hook. The Grey is also suitable for shallow lake fishing up to 20 metres or so with mid-depth presentation for fish like rudd, skimmers and crucian carp.

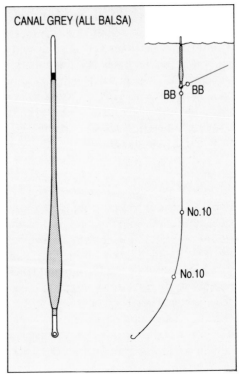

CANAL GREY (ALL BALSA)

BB   BB

No.10

No.10

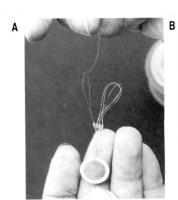

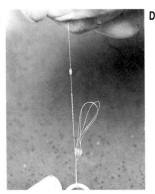

A   B   C   D

Sliders

Sooner or later you will want to fish a swim which is too deep for conventional float tackle. For instance, if your rod is 13ft then depths beyond four metres (12ft) are difficult to fish effectively with a fixed float. In swims where there is more than 14ft of water you'd find it impossible.

The solution is to switch to a slider float. There are two designs for deep water—the bottom-end only, waggler style float for stillwaters and the double-eyed balsa for running swims. The waggler slider is normally bodied and may also be semi-weighted in the stem. Usually, these floats are fished with a bulk weight positioned approximately 1 to 1.25 metres (3-4ft) from the hook with a No.4 or 6 dropper-shot midway between bulk and hook. A small shot is also fixed a foot above the bulk weights to stop the float from sliding and tangling on the cast.

SLIDING FLOAT STOP KNOT

These floats have either a tiny wire eye at the base or a small swivel through which the line is free running. The float is stopped at the required depth you want to fish by a sliding float knot. The alternative is to use a rubber sliding float stop which is less obtrusive than a knot. This tiny stop is slipped on the reel line before whichever design of slider you choose. In very deep swims, it will wind on the reel and will not impede casting as it travels through the rod rings.

Once a bottom-end slider has been set up it can be fished in a similar fashion to a normal waggler.

The top and bottom slider is basically an all-balsa float with an extra side eye added so the reel line slides unhindered until it is braked by a stop knot.

Again, it is used in water too deep for your rod with identical shotting to the bottom-ender. For close-in work, it is practical to fish this float on stillwaters if the wind or drift isn't too bad. But really this design is meant for flowing water.

If the float moves through the swim too fast, change to a heavier model. The extra weight of a bigger float slows its progress downstream. Another use for top and bottom sliders is in overgrown swims where an overhead or sideways cast is impossible. You can flick the slider out underarm to quite a distance.

How to use a rubber float stop.

A. Feed the reel line through the wire loop holding the rubber stop.
B. Push the rubber stop towards the end of the retaining wire.
C. Clasp the line as shown and slide the stop off the loop and on to the nylon. Withdraw loose end of the line from rubber stop.
D. Move the stop up line to the required depth for fishing the slider.

Below: A bottom-end slider rig for stillwaters.

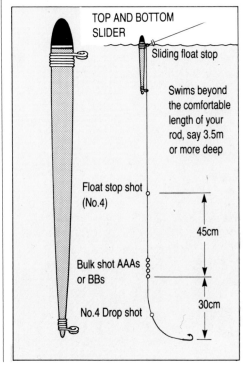

TOP AND BOTTOM SLIDER

Sliding float stop

Swims beyond the comfortable length of your rod, say 3.5m or more deep

Float stop shot (No.4)

45cm

Bulk shot AAAs or BBs

30cm

No.4 Drop shot

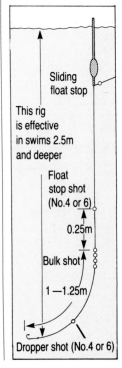

Sliding float stop

This rig is effective in swims 2.5m and deeper

Float stop shot (No.4 or 6)

0.25m

Bulk shot

1—1.25m

Dropper shot (No.4 or 6)

ATTRACTORS

The chief hookbaits

The plain white maggot has always been the freshwater bait in greatest demand but it needs to be in tip-top condition. Fresh bait is easily recognisable by a black feed spot beneath the skin and the maggot should be soft rather than rubbery to the touch.

There is considerable scope for experiment with a range of coloured maggots. Favourites are red, bronze and yellow although green and blue are not unheard of! Dyed baits increase your options at the bankside. A change to a coloured bait frequently produces extra fish on hard fished waters where whites are widely used.

Some species also seem to have definite colour preferences. This is unclear ground, scientifically, because fish are only supposed to see in monochrome. But match anglers wouldn't be without bronze maggots for roach and chub or dark red ones when after tench and perch. Colour is something each angler must experiment with for himself.

Maggot types

Shop maggots are not restricted to large whites. **Pinkies** are about half their size and as the name suggests they have a pinkish tinge in their natural state. They're

Lively, well fed maggots give you a head start compared with those fishing stale bait. Pack a riddle to remove all traces of debris.

favourites with matchmen and canal anglers for catching small fish on light tackle with small hooks. Like big maggots, pinkies are sold in their natural form or dyed red, bronze and sometimes yellow.

Squatts

Then there are squatts which were once exclusively used by bream anglers in groundbait. The squatt is half the size again of the pinkie and being so small it is less mobile in water and does not bury itself in the bottom-mud out of sight of the fish.

Squatts have now found their way out of the groundbait bowl and on to the hook as a frontline bait. Canal anglers were responsible for its promotion and they rate it very highly as a prime bait and as loose feed. Scaled down tackle is a must with the squatt.

Most squatts come as whites stored in damp, red-brick sand. Lately, there has been a trend to feed squatts dyed red to simulate the bloodworm on venues where this tiny worm is banned. But nothing can really compare with the potency of the bright red bloodworm itself which is the larvae of midge found in massive quantities in the bottom mud of many fisheries.

Gozzers

The other maggot type is the gozzer which cannot be reared commercially. It must be home-bred by the angler in a medium-sized heart from the butcher's shop. Producing gozzers is a fiddling business but the end result is a much softer skinned maggot than is obtainable commercially and they're excellent for bream.

To turn out your own gozzers, you'll need to start the process ten days before your planned fishing trip. First, make several cuts through the heart without completely separating the sections and place it on a bed of clean bran in a large tin or similar sized container with a lid. Leave the lid slightly open or make a hole in it big enough for a fly to enter and lay its eggs in the heart — a process known as the blow.

Put the container outside in a shady, dry spot such as under thick bushes in the

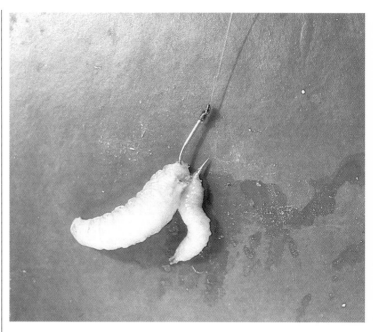

This photograph shows the size difference between a standard white (left) and pinkie.

garden or in a garden shed with an open window. After a couple of days in mild weather there should be several patches of eggs on the cuts in the heart. But you only require two or three clusters of eggs otherwise there will be too many maggots feeding on the meat and the gozzers will be very small. Scrape any surplus blows off the heart with a knife.

Next, wrap the heart quite loosely in newspaper and cover with fresh bran to help prevent smells. After six or seven days the gozzers are ready for riddling off and placing in fresh, slightly dampened bran in a bait box to stop them escaping.

Improving shop maggots

If you haven't got the time or facilities to produce your own special bait, it's still possible to enhance shop-bought bait. A small maggot riddle and some fresh sawdust, even a sprinkling of fine maize meal, can work wonders with indifferent bait.

Maize or bran will make maggots a lot softer to the touch if you store them in a cool spot in a large, open-topped container. Soft maggots bring more positive bites. The only time when tough skinned, older bait should be considered is in very cold water which makes fresh maggots stretch very quickly.

Single maggots must be mounted so they wriggle away from the point of the hook.

Flavourings for maggots

There are sound reasons for giving maggots extra appeal with flavouring. If you smoke, it's possible to transfer the taint to the maggot which the fish can detect. And if the bait is warm, an unpleasant smell of ammonia is given off which also repels the fish. If nothing else, the application of a pleasant flavour to the bait masks out any of these negative smells and boosts confidence. In practical terms, it doesn't seem unreasonable to assume that a bait which leaks an attractive scent trail in the water helps draw fish into the vicinity. This must be true in very murky water where baits on the bottom are less visible.

Overall, colouring and flavouring of maggots will broaden your options. It's reassuring to know that you've got something else up your sleeve if the first choice bait doesn't work. Top anglers may be supremely confident with just a couple of pints of white maggots — they have got the experience to make them work 90 percent of the time. If you're lacking in know-how carrying a choice of baits helps boost your chances. Anyway, it's a fair bet that the expert will have the odd bottle of flavouring hidden away in his tackle box just in case!

Mounting maggots on the hook

Even the most succulent maggots in the world will be instantly ruined if hooked incorrectly. The best way to mount a single maggot is through the tiny flap of skin at the tail or blunt end. This doesn't impede the movement of the bait and if anything makes the maggot wriggle even more enticingly. Make certain you don't mask the point of the hook with the maggot otherwise fish will get bumped off on the strike.

Generally, you should use fine wire hooks ranging from 18s to 24s for single maggot. Fish double-maggot when after bigger fish to help deter small fry, possibly with a heavier forged hook down to a 14. A cluster of maggots can be mounted on an even bigger hook to help disguise its size for barbel and carp.

Keeping casters fresh

If maggots are kept for several days they eventually turn into chrysalids. At first, these are an attractive light bronze colour but they turn a deeper brown and finally almost black. In their lighter condition, chrysalids sink but as soon as they go dark they float. In their sinking stage they are known as **casters** which are a brilliant big-fish bait.

It's time consuming and wasteful on maggots to try and turn enough casters for your own use. Better tackle shops sell them ready-packed in airtight plastic bags but they're such a popular bait that they must be ordered several days in advance of your fishing trip. Few shops sell them

off the shelf because they turn so quickly.

Casters are best stored in a fridge but the bag must be opened to allow fresh air to enter every eight hours. This will prevent them turning grey and dying or getting burn marks from the plastic bag. When replacing the air, leave the bag open for just a couple of minutes and no longer otherwise they'll quickly blacken off and turn into floaters.

Are casters worth this much effort? Well, long experience with them has more than proved their effectiveness for loose feeding or mixing with groundbait. Casters never wriggle away on the bottom at the point where they are introduced and unlike large maggots they won't get buried in the mud. They fall through the water at varying rates of descent which is very tempting to the fish and this also makes it easier to disguise your hookbait among the loose offerings.

The ability to completely hide a hook inside a caster helps considerably in clear water. Quality fish will often seize a caster on days when they won't touch a maggot. It's a bait worth fussing over!

Double caster is more effective for fish like chub, barbel, carp, bream and tench and can be fished on a strong, forged hook pattern. Use sizes between 14 and 18 inclusive for double baits with finer wire 16s, 18s or 20s for single caster.

Versatile bread

Maggots and casters are good standard baits but there are plenty of other possibilities and bread rates as one of the most versatile. It can be fished in crust and flake form on big hooks or as paste and pellets compressed from a punch with tiny hooks.

The correct way to hook a single caster is to bury the hook until it is almost completely hidden.

Freshly turned casters — crisp and certain catchers on many waters.

A large lump of fresh flake trundled downriver in winter has probably accounted for more big roach over the years than any other bait.

Crust and flake

Surface fished crust is particularly liked by carp and chub and a slow-sinking piece in weedy swims will rest gently on underwater foliage or muddy bottoms without disappearing out of sight. Depending on its size, a piece of flake can be used on a fair range of larger hooks for a wide cross-section of species. Most fish will take a chunk of bread at some time.

If necessary, it's feasible to step up to as big a hook as a forged size 2 when fishing crust, although a 4, 6 or 8 is normally adequate. The same applies to flake where a 10 or 12 is suitable for roach and bream fishing.

Paste

Paste is presented on all sizes from 2s to 16s but don't go any smaller otherwise it will tend to fall off on the cast. To overcome that limitation, matchmen developed the breadpunch with multi-sized heads for compressing and cutting out tiny pellets of bread from a sliced white loaf. The advantage of this method is that the bait is transferred to the hook without being touched eliminating any possibility of tainting.

Flavouring

While it is unusual to flavour visual baits like floating crust and flake, it is common to spice up paste or breadpunch. Paste is best made from a decrusted, stale white loaf. Slightly dampen the dry interior crumb and squeeze out in a dry cloth. The ball of damp bread is then kneaded into the right texture to stay on the hook.

At this stage you can add some flavouring. Soft cheese is a popular addition and should be kneaded in to slightly harden up the paste. Custard powder is another good firming agent.

With breadpunch it is easier to carry a

How to work with a breadpunch.
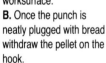
A. Punches make it easy to produce compact pellets of bread for hard fished venues where small hooks are a must. All you'll need for a day's fishing is a few slices of fresh bread and a hard, flat surface on which to work. Select the appropriate size of punch and press down vertically into the bread until you can feel it has penetrated through to your makeshift worksurface.
B. Once the punch is neatly plugged with bread withdraw the pellet on the hook.
C. Make sure the pellet sits on the bend of the hook with the point exposed.

A

B

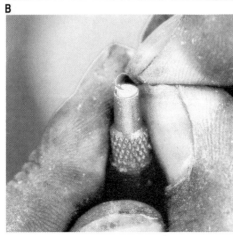

C

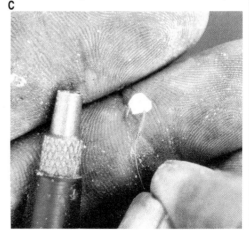

small bottle of flavouring and to dunk the bait into it after it has been put on the hook. Flavours worth considering include banana, cheese and vanilla.

Worms

Worms will trick numerous species of fish but this bait is chiefly associated with perch, eels, tench, bream and chub. There are several types you can use ranging from the big lobworm found on grass lawns at night — usually when the weather is damp and mild — to the more easily collectable brandlings and redworms.

Lobworms

Lobworms are often fished whole on big hooks for chub and tench while the tail end makes a good mouthful on middle-sized hooks for roach, perch and eels.

Brandlings or redworms

If you buy worms from a tackle shop they're likely to be brandlings or red-worms. There's something of a stigma attached to brandlings because they ooze a repulsive looking body fluid when impaled on the hook. But take no notice of other anglers' objections. The brandling will catch you plenty of fish and there are occasions in summer droughts when they're the only worm obtainable anyway.

Use brandlings on an 8 or 10 hook if they're on the large side, going down to a pattern between 12 and 18 depending on bait size. They're particularly well liked by tench, perch and bream. Canal anglers sometimes chop up these worms into tiny pieces on hard venues for gudgeon, small perch and ruffe.

Redworms tend to be small and lively which has persuaded many a fine roach to the net. Bream, tench and perch also find them a tasty snack. It's a good worm for chopping up in quantity for introducing into groundbait when you are fishing for tench and bream. A hook size between 10 and 14 is preferred for these species while smaller bream will fall to a redworm lightly hooked in the head on a 16 or 18. Sometimes a cocktail bait of worm tipped off with caster or red maggot works very much better.

Seed baits

Hemp and tares

There are three popular seed baits associated with summer and to a lesser extent autumn. These are hemp, tares and sweetcorn. But the drawing power of hemp is so powerful that anglers carry on using it as loose feed well into the winter months, normally with maggots or casters. In the summer and autumn, hemp is a superb roach attractor both as loose feed and on the hook. But it must be introduced and fished skilfully to bring results.

Preparing hemp and tares

A pint of cooked hemp is sufficient for a full day's fishing and preparation is simple. Tip a pint of seeds into a large saucepan and cover with water. Then bring to the boil with the lid removed. Once the water reaches boiling point, turn the heat down and let the hemp simmer for 30 minutes with the saucepan lid not quite covering the pan. Check periodically to ensure the water doesn't evaporate completely. If there's not enough water covering the seeds after ten minutes or so, top up the level with an extra cupful.

The bait is ready when small, white shoots emerge on most of the seeds. Rinse off with cold water through a strainer to prevent over cooking. If overdone, hemp splits open too much and is impossible to keep on the hook. Tares are often used on the hook with hemp as loose feed and the combination works very well. The tare is four times larger than hemp when cooked. It is much softer skinned and impales on the hook more easily. The fish seem to home in on this bigger offering

among the smaller grains of loose fed hemp. The tare can be used in its natural light brown state or soaked in soda to blacken off and simulate hemp. The simplest way to prepare tares is to add a handful to the hemp while it is cooking. That will be ample for a session.

Baiting-up

With hemp as hookbait, a 16 or 18 hook is recommended, pushing the bend into the split where the tiny white shoot emerges. For tares, a 14 or 16 is about right, usually just lightly skin-hooking the bait. If the fish are a little shy, push the hook into the tare where a slight seam runs around one side. This only leaves part of the shank visible.

Always make sure the point of the hook is just protruding with hemp and tares to ease the task of setting it home on the strike. It can prove a devil of a job if the point is buried in the bait.

When fed correctly, hemp is capable of mesmerising fish like roach, chub and

Above: Always leave the hookpoint standing proud of the tare.

Right: The usual brown tare treated with soda to create an all-black hookbait. Fish will mistake it for any one of a number of aquatic creatures. Here is a mixture of treated and untreated tares.

Ready-packed boilies were originally developed for carp but several other species have found them to their liking.

barbel into a feeding frenzy. With roach and chub, this means feeding a few grains on every cast. The bait is not always instant-acting. It might take several hours to work up a swim but it's worth the effort.

Once fish go for the bait, there's no stopping them. You'll be in for a hectic time!

Hemp tactics for barbel are rather different. A large carpet is laid on the bottom and sometimes it takes half-a-gallon or more to pull in the fish. But once the barbel are in the swim, the hemp will hold them for long periods.

Sweetcorn

This is a summer bait linked with tench, bream and carp on stillwaters but it will also tempt chub, barbel and roach on river venues. A 10, 12 or 14 gilt coloured, eyed hook is best and a strong hooklength is advised because the bites are often quite savage.

Sweetcorn can be floatfished on an overdepth rig or legered with an open-ended swimfeeder which is preferred to a straight leger these days. A recent successful innovation is to dye corn a deep red colour. Powdered sweetcorn flavouring is also gaining popularity as a groundbait ingredient.

Boilies

Once it was discovered that carp would actively search out man-made baits packed with proteins, the nation's kitchens were beseiged by anglers who previously couldn't boil an egg. Bait recipes were exchanged and results compared over many seasons until the boilie became the universal bait for carp. But it was a hard slog mixing up milk-based products, flavourings and eggs let alone the boiling and hand rolling. A session in the kitchen producing prebaiting supplies and hookbaits could easily take a whole evening. There had to be a better way.

Sure enough, a whole industry finally grew up around the boilie and commercially made packs have made it unnecessary for anybody to spend time sweating over a hot stove. The choice of colours and flavours is mammoth. Incredibly exotic offerings range from savoury sea food blends to sweet tropical fruits. Blends like Salmon Supreme, Atlantic Prawn and Cocktail Fruit have sold in their millions.

Types of boilie

Ready-made boilies are sold frozen or in six month, shelf-life packs. There are also neutral boilies which you spray with the flavour of your choice using an atomiser and then leave overnight in a sealed plastic bag.

On heavily fished waters the fish might become preoccupied on a particular flavour or colour and ignore everything else. It's helpful, therefore, to investigate the taking-baits just in case this has happened. But more often, boilies will produce runs very quickly on waters where they are being fished regularly. On the other hand, if the fishery has never seen a boilie then it could take some time for the fish to adjust and become weaned on the bait.

Choosing your boilie

How do you go about choosing the best boilie from the hundreds on offer? The tackle dealer might have the answer if he knows the water you intend to fish. But you'll probably identify the best selling lines anyway by the gaps on the shelves! Having discovered a couple of good flavours and colours, the next question is how to get an edge over the other anglers. It stands to reason that if there are 20 other anglers on the lake, the odds are going to be 20-1 against you catching a good fish unless you're fortunate enough to find a hotspot vacant.

Let's assume most carp are falling to a red bait with Salmon Supreme the No.1 tempter. You can hedge your bets by going for a red boilie that's also savoury, say King Prawn, or another sea food recipe. That way you're fishing an almost identical bait to the one that's catching which should be sufficient to interest the fish. And because you're offering a slightly different concoction, there's a good possibility that you'll pull in fish that have grown suspicious of the Salmon Supreme baits.

Another confidence boosting option is to take a successful bait on a midweek session when few other anglers are about. With most of the water to yourself you can draw fish from a much wider range.

Boilies are not exclusive to carp fishing — they will catch several other species. Some big hauls of tench have fallen to red boilies in a variety of savoury flavours. Bream seem to prefer lighter coloured and sweeter yellows and oranges. Honey, vanilla and some fruit based aromas go down well.

One final word of advice on flavours is to keep an eye on seasonal changes. Some flavours certainly appear to be more effective at given times of the year. Stick to fruity sweet flavours in the warmer months and switch to savoury boilies from autumn onwards and you'll be on the right track.

Tutti Frutti, Caribbean Cocktail and Tropical Mango are good off the shelf summer purchases. Salmon Supreme, King Prawn and Seafood catch plenty once the weather becomes cooler.

Groundbait mixes

Some very complicated groundbait mixes were around long before boilies made their mark and in many ways the thinking behind them is very similar. Matchmen soon discovered that complex Continental mixes seemed to draw and hold fish very well, particularly when fishing at close range with the pole.

To put groundbait into perspective, the most basic form is white or brown breadcrumb. White on its own goes a little stodgy when mixed with water. But brown turns fluffy and produces a nice cloud when introduced into the swim in the right manner. The two can also be mixed to achieve different consistencies.

Fish may be attracted by groundbait either visually or by its aroma. This gives the angler the choice of drawing fish to his hookbait by a visually attractive cloud effect or introducing a feed mix which will hopefully hold the fish while they eat their way to his hookbait.

Groundbait is a good attractor when loose feeding fails. There is a limit to the distance you can throw or catapult loose feed and that's often a drawback. Sometimes, it will go unnoticed simply because the fish are not resident in the swim. But groundbait in cloud form is much more visible and as fish are naturally inquisitive creatures they'll want to investigate. It is quite normal for water to become coloured by wave action, extra rain or boats which stir up debris. Fish associate these disturbances with finding food.

Another use for groundbait is as a carrier to deposit loose feed greater distances. And heavy groundbait will hold on the bottom of fast flowing swims when loose feed is swept away.

Continental groundbaits

Breadcrumb is used countrywide as groundbait but it is easy to overfeed the fish. Crumb swells to twice its size in water and fish are quickly filled up. That's where European anglers have been very clever, formulating mixes which contain very little, if any, bread feed. Instead, they rely heavily on non-absorbing ingredients like crushed hemp and overcooked biscuit flour. Bland flours like ground walnut, peanut and coconut are also incorporated and there can be up to a dozen ingredients in the more successful Continental mixes.

We are just beginning to learn the true capabilities of Continental groundbait recipes although they have been very popular in this country for a decade. This is because in most cases they were not designed for our waters or our way of fishing and have had to be adapted. Many matchmen, club anglers and pleasure anglers now mix these recipes together for particular situations or dilute them with breadcrumb.

On the tackle shop shelves you'll find Continental groundbaits developed for particular species of fish and with very

different consistencies. Some bind well, others give a lovely cloudy effect. Some are even recommended for use with certain baits like bloodworm, maggots or casters.

Pick of the Continental mixes

To help you achieve a greater understanding of continental groundbaits, here's a guide to some of the best selling brands. Beware! You may find it difficult to decipher some of the instructions on the packets.

Magic

This mixture is coloured red, yellow or plain. A good general purpose groundbait for roach, skimmers and bigger bream in the plain colour with baits like maggots, casters, bloodworm and pinkies.

Mien Futter

A sweet smelling bream and small fish mix which works well with maggots and bloodworm on canals and lakes.

Sensas 2,000

A stodgy brown binder added to other groundbaits to hold them together for feeding at distance or in heavy flows.

Expo

A dark red, big fish groundbait which can be mixed dry and fluffy with little water or into heavy consistency with extra wetting. Teams with casters, red maggots and worms for tench, big roach and small carp.

Secret

This is a heavy river style groundbait which will deposit bloodworm, jokers (see page 109) and most other small baits hard on the bottom in fast currents. Works for most species.

Beet

A cloudy small fish mix for on-the-drop fishing in lakes and canals for roach and skimmer bream.

A red groundbait mix caled Expo from the Marcel van den Eynde range which works wonders when after tench.

All Round and Super Cup

These are fine cloud mixes for clear water conditions. They are best mixed very dry and give a very soft cloud effect which attracts small fish when usbed with baits like bloodworm, pinkies, squatts and breadpunch.

Kaaster

A very good big bream groundbait. Binds well for feeding a mixture of squatts, casters and chopped worms at distance or in heavy flow.

X21

French, grey coloured recipe which is good when used with bloodworm. It always seems to draw skimmer bream if they are in the area.

Plumm

A very light and sweet smelling bait. Another on-the-drop style groundbait to be fished with maggots, pinkies, squatts and bloodworm on canals and shallow lakes for fish like skimmers and roach.

Picardie

A curry flavoured mix designed for gudgeon and it really works! Bloodworm or pinkies are the best baits.

Alga Rouge

A pre-dampened groundbait dark red in colour. An excellent attractor on hard, clear canal venues for perch, gudgeon, skimmers and roach.

English groundbait

English companies are now making up similar recipes but you'll have no problems with these as their uses are fully and clearly explained on the packets. If a lot of fish are expected, mix up some breadcrumb with the Continental groundbait to make it go further. When the weather becomes colder and bites are less frequent, switch to a more concentrated Continental mix — but introduce it more sparingly.

Catapults

A catapult is needed to feed loose offerings, boilies and groundbait at distance. A well designed, loose feed 'pult increases feeding range up to 30 metres if the wind is right. On canals and small rivers this is a big advantage because you can spray casters or maggots right across to the far bank.

Boilie catapults fire a bait up to 60 metres or more. Stepping up in fire-power there's the Black Widow with its wrist support which blasts a single boilie 100 metres!

Finally, a good groundbait catapult is a must for bream on large, open gravel pits or big, sluggish rivers where the fishing range is frequently 40 metres or more. Make sure you pick the right gauge of elastic and also check the pouch is rigid enough not to break up the ball of groundbait.

Bait chart

Bait	Species	Recommended hook size/pattern
Maggots	Barbel,bleak,bream,carp chub,dace,eels,gudgeon, perch,roach,rudd,ruffe, tench.	Single:18-24,fine wire. Double:14-18,forged. Multiple:8-12,forged.
Casters	Barbel,bream,carp,chub, dace,eels,roach,rudd, tench.	Single:16-20,fine wire. Double:14-18,forged. Multiple:10-12,forged.
Pinkies	Bleak,skimmer bream,dace, eels,gudgeon,perch,roach, rudd,ruffe,tench.	Single:20-24,fine wire. Double:20,fine or forged.
Squatts	Bleak,bream(and skimmers), dace,gudgeon,perch,roach, rudd,ruffe,tench.	Single:22-24,fine wire. Double:20-22,fine wire.
Worms	Barbel,bream,carp,chub, eels,perch,roach, ruffe,tench.	Lobs:2-12,forged. Brandlings:8-16,forged. Reds:14-18,fine wire.
Bloodworms	Bleak,bream,skimmers,gudgeon, perch,roach,rudd,ruffe,tench.	Single:20-26,fine wire. Double:18-24,fine wire.
Breadpunch	Bleak,skimmer bream, gudgeon,roach,rudd.	16-24,fine wire.
Breadflake and crust	Barbel,bream,carp, chub,roach,tench.	Large pieces:2-12,forged. Small:12-16,fine wire.
Luncheon meat	Barbel,carp,chub,tench.	Large pieces:4-10,forged. Small:12-16,forged.
Boilies	Barbel,bream,carp, chub,tench.	Standard:6-10,forged. Mini:10-14,forged.
Hemp	Barbel,chub,dace, roach,rudd.	Big fish:14-18,forged. Roach,etc:14-20,fine wire.
Tares	Barbel,bream,carp, chub,roach.	Big fish:12-18,forged. Roach,etc:14-18,fine wire.
Sweetcorn	Barbel,bream,carp,chub, roach,rudd,tench.	Single:12-16,forged. Multiple:8-12,forged

LEGERING

With the exception of specimen hunters, the majority of coarse anglers invest most effort in floatfishing. But certain situations call for a drastic change of tackle and if you ignore the signs you won't catch any fish.

The float should be stripped from the line in favour of a single leger weight or swimfeeder when the fish are beyond floatfishing range and you can't tempt them closer. Another signal to change is if the flow or drift prevents you holding the float tackle stationary when the fish demand a bait fished that way.

With legering techniques it is possible to more than double the range of float tackle and in flowing water you can stop a bait hard on the bottom at distances that would defeat the float.

The straight leger restores the balance of tackle presentation back in the angler's favour when the float is in trouble. But the swimfeeder will often do the job just as well if not better.

There are two basic types of feeder popularly known as **open-end** and **blockend**. Both are manufactured from clear or coloured plastic and are perforated with exit holes to release bait. The difference between the two is that the open-ended model is used for groundbait and the blockend purely with loose feed like maggots, hemp and casters.

Cage feeders are a new development and consist simply of a latticed metal framework in the shape of a cylindrical plastic feeder through and around which the groundbait is moulded.

Open-ended swimfeeders

The open-end feeder is made in several sizes with corresponding increases in weight loading and each takes different amounts of feed. Extra weight can be added with purpose-made leads which clip on the feeder body or fit underneath existing weights.

The open-end design usually has a short nylon loop at one end to which an American swivel link is clipped. The reel line is

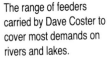

The range of feeders carried by Dave Coster to cover most demands on rivers and lakes.

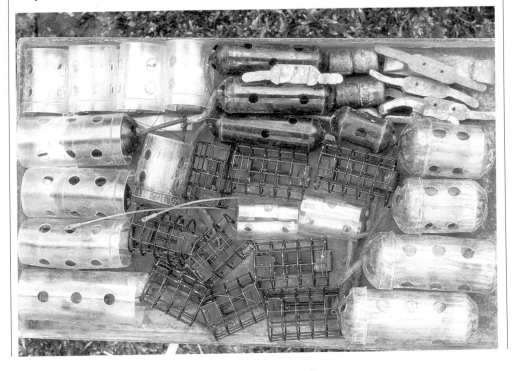

then threaded through the swivel and the feeder stopped with a splitshot or leger stop. Below this goes the hooklength.

There is little need to introduce extra links or to cover the nylon loop on this swimfeeder with silicone tubing to prevent the hooklength tangling. The rig is relatively problem-free.

Open-enders can be filled with groundbait alone — pure crumb is the favourite when fishing bread on the hook — or with a combination of groundbait and loose offerings like casters, squatts, hemp and pinkies. The loose bait is mixed into the groundbait and pressed inside the feeder or compressed in the centre with retaining plugs of groundbait at either end.

Lately, Continental groundbaits have become very popular for this type of feeder fishing. Their excellent binding qualities hold in loose feed very well for long casting.

Blockend feeders

Blockend or closed feeders have two end caps. The bottom one is normally permanently fixed while the top cap is removable to allow the feeder to be filled. Blockends offer more resistance to flowing water than open-ended models and tend to roll before settling. This can cause the hooklength to twist around the nylon attachment loop on the feeder. The answer is to slip a short length of silicone tubing over the nylon link then there is nothing for the hook to catch on during the cast or when the rig hits bottom. The tendency of the blockend to tangle has resulted in some manufacturers incorporating short links made of plastic which solves the problem to some extent. Other models come complete with a swivel which is moulded in the top cap of the feeder.

Blockends are usually filled with maggots which gradually filter out of the exit holes ensuring a steady trickle of loose offerings are spread around the hookbait.

Caster and hempseed make another good combination in the feeder with caster or maggot on the hook. Like open-enders, these designs are manufactured in varying sizes ranging from tiny feeder-

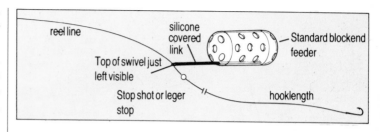

links which are fished with small baits like pinkies through to the big blockends for piling large amounts of maggots in the swim when big catches are anticipated.

The swimfeeder is a good method because it guarantees that loose feed or groundbait will be distributed precisely where it is wanted around the hookbait. It's a deadly technique even in the hands of a novice angler.

But it's not completely foolproof. The thinking angler will get excellent results with the feeder if he moderates its use to keep the fish in the swim. Carry on crashing feeder after feeder on the heads of a shoal and you'll soon spook them unless they're in a rare feeding frenzy.

Generally, it's best to give the feeder a break every now and then and switch to a straight leger until the swim needs further topping up with bait. As a rough guide, use the feeder until the swim comes alive then alternate with an Arlesey bomb, the priority being to keep the bites coming.

There are, of course, venues and types of swim where the straight leger will outscore the swimfeeder. Think twice before slinging out a feeder in shallow, clear lake water or hard fished canal venues. It will do more damage than good! The feeder is also more likely to spook big fish like bream in stillwaters than it might on flowing rivers.

It's really a case of commonsense. If you can feed accurately without a feeder and present the hookbait in unison with the feed, then do so. The swimfeeder's big drawback is that it creates disturbance. It should only be used as a last resort in shallow stillwaters, canals with flow or small shallow rivers — if all the other options have failed to produce results.

It is not so critical on deeper stillwaters and rivers or at long range where its impact is lessened.

A reasonably tangle-proof blockend feeder rig. The reel line is threaded directly through a single swivel which is partly covered by silicone tubing, or an American swivel link may be attached to this first.

The swingtip is extremely
sensitive when correctly
set up.

Bite detection

There are several ways of interpreting
bites when legering and each method has
its strengths and weaknesses. The leading
indicators are swingtips, quivertips and
springtips. Which you choose depends on
the swim, weather conditions and target
species.

Swingtips

Swingtips are not as popular as they were
in the past but still play an important role
in modern angling. They're often associated with bream on still or slightly flowing
waters where the method can be unbeat-
able.

Bream are notoriously fickle and will
spend some time playing with a bait before deciding to take it. The low resistance
offered by a swingtip is much less likely
to scare a fish in this sort of mood.

Another advantage of the swingtip is the
wider arc of striking power it affords when
fishing at distance. The rod is positioned
pointing towards the end tackle instead
of the 45 degree angle that's required with
the quivertip.

Swingtips are sold in varying materials
and lengths ranging from 12.5 or 15 centimetres (five or six inches) up to about
30 centimetres (a foot or so). They can
be made from Sarkandas reed, cane, plastic or even carbon.

For the most positive bite indication, a
length of 20 to 25 centimetres (eight or ten
inches) is about right for normal conditions, using a swingtip made from a light
material. To counteract drift, wind or
flow, light swingtips must be fitted with
special pre-formed, rigid rubber connec-
tors. These give different degrees of flexibility and are pre-set at the desired 45
degree angle.

If a medium length swingtip is still unstable despite changing to the stiffest rubber
connector, the next step is to wrap lead
wire around the end of the tip or switch
to a longer, heavier model. Experienced
swingtip anglers sometimes use custom-
made tips with reverse tapers up to 45
centimetres (18in) long to increase weight
and stability. Specials can be made from
thicker fibre-glass or solid carbon. As long
as the tip is just heavy enough to balance
out against flow, drift or wind it is doubtful if the additional weight makes a great
deal of difference to a fish that's mouthing

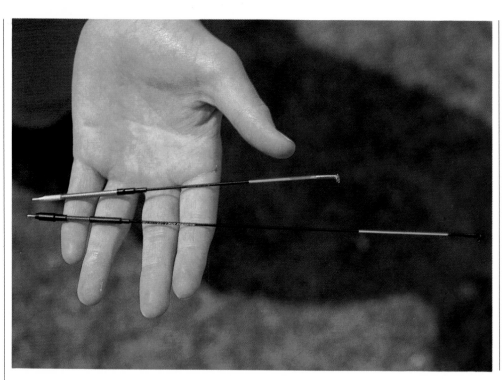

Standard springtip and adjustable model which doubles as a quiver by pushing the tip back through the spring.
If your tip bends before the spring comes into play then buy a new one! The spring must collapse first on the bite otherwise you might as well resort to a straight quivertip.

Below: Setting-up your swingtip.

the bait.

The weight limit is reached when the tip starts to affect the rod's action on the cast. Long swingtips should also have one or possibly two intermediate eyes to prevent tangles and to ease line flow.

The rod must be supported by a minimum of two rests when swingtipping to keep the sensitive tip rock steady. Make sure the rests are correctly spaced to prevent any part of the rod drooping. Sag will take a great deal of power out of the rod's action on the strike. In rough conditions it is not out of the question to use three rests to stop the wind from making false movements on the tip.

When fishing at distances over 40 metres it is probably best to point the rod in its rests towards the terminal tackle for maximum striking power. But for shorter range fishing, the rod's angle to the end tackle is increased, especially when the wind shakes the rod tip. If you can tuck the rod out of the main force of the wind or shelter it in any way, this is all to the good.

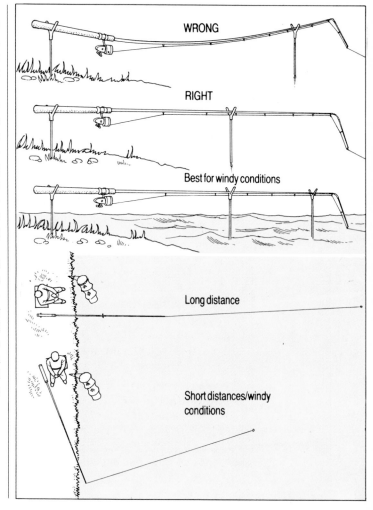

WRONG

RIGHT

Best for windy conditions

Long distance

Short distances/windy conditions

Quivertips

The quivertip is Britain's No.1 bite indicator. The most convenient model is the screw-in version which fits a threaded top eye. These can be fitted to most leger rods or even shorter match rods if required.

Screw-in indicators are available in different lengths, tapers and test curves ranging from very stiff river models down to long, extra fine canal or stillwater designs. If your rod has a threaded top eye, it is advisable to carry several different strength quivers to deal with varying flow rates.

Many manufacturers are now producing leger blanks with two, three or four interchangeable tips which slot into the main rod. This is a superior system because there's a better relationship between the indicator and the rod. A more gradual step-down from the blank itself to the finer tip is achieved.

The other option is to buy a rod with a built-in quivertip but you've got to be very sure of the rod and its intended use. This rod will probably be more powerful and robust but you'll lose the versatility of the

other options unless, of course, you can afford two or three specialist rods.

The most common fault when quivertipping is poor positioning of the rod. Many anglers simply get themselves comfortable and drop the rod in rests without giving much thought to where it should be pointing.

Nothing is gained by pointing the rod directly at the end tackle. If there's only a small angle or no angle at all where the line leaves the tip ring on the quiver, then bites won't register correctly.

On fast flowing waters, a stiffish actioned tip must be used because the current would pull round a finer one too severely for bites to show up. The rod needs to be positioned quite high to get as much of the line out of the water as possible to prevent the flow dragging the end rig out of place.

Usually, it's preferable if the rod is pointing downstream in this situation. But you can point it upstream if the swim makes this impossible by a few modifications.

The bow method

This brings us to an interesting point with quivertipping. You can actually get away with too fine a tip in a fast flow and overcome the problems of poor bite indication. This is achieved by feeding line into the current to reduce the effect of flow or water pressure. This method is called fishing the bow. It's a brilliant technique if you can balance the tackle because the fish don't feel such heavy resistance when they pick up the hookbait. Normally, they hook themselves!

Basically, the bow method entails using lighter gear all round including a feeder that's barely heavy enough to hold bottom. Once it has landed in the swim, line is fed out into the flow. Up to several yards can be released while the rod is being placed in the rests. The line should be fed in a downstream direction but if it must be upstream then more is released to compensate.

This system is more sensitive than tight lining in flow. Really you are making the current work for you. The water pressure

Below and right: Today many rod manufacturers are producing custom-made quivertip rods that take up to three or four slot-in quivers. In many ways this is preferable to screw-in quivertips as a better action is achieved.

Imbalance on screw-in design

Smoother curve on slot-in type quiver

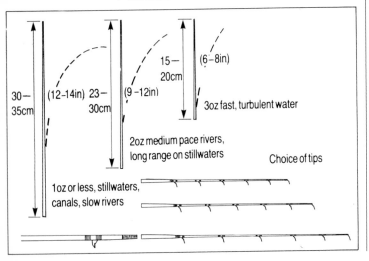

30—35cm (1oz or less, stillwaters, canals, slow rivers)

(12-14in) 23—30cm (2oz medium pace rivers, long range on stillwaters)

(9-12in)

15—20cm (6-8in) 3oz fast, turbulent water

Choice of tips

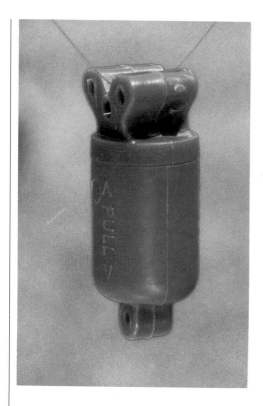

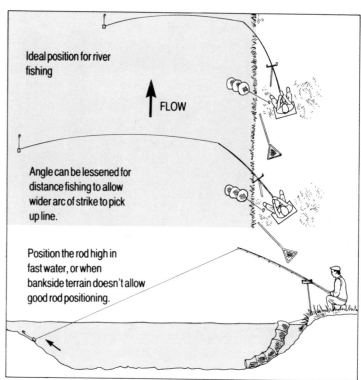

Ideal position for river fishing

FLOW

Angle can be lessened for distance fishing to allow wider arc of strike to pick up line.

Position the rod high in fast water, or when bankside terrain doesn't allow good rod positioning.

on the large bow of line causes the finer quivertip to pull round but not overmuch because of the line feeding process which eases the pressure.

Let's assume you've got the feeder size right and it's just holding against the bow. When a fish pulls on the hooklength the balance is upset and the feeder rolls downstream — pulled by all that line in the water. The weight of the line and feeder suddenly being released results in the quivertip dropping back sharply and at the same time sets the hook! All you have to do is pick up the rod and lift into the fish.

The line needs to be kept at an angle of 45 degrees to the rod tip when quivertipping on both rivers and stillwaters. But at great distances, the angle can be reduced to allow for the greater arc of strike needed to set the hook.

Stillwaters or gently flowing rivers require much finer, longer tips otherwise the fish feel resistance and just rattle the tip without giving any hittable bites. Here it's better to position the rod low with most of the line submerged but again always point the rod downstream of any flow or drift.

Another trick in fast flow is to hold the rod in the right hand and feel for bites on the line with the left just above the reel. This is called **touch legering** and is surprisingly sensitive to the slightest pluck from a shy fish.

Springtips

The springtip is made like a quiver but is fitted with a coiled spring just above the screw-in attachment for the rod. Some models serve as dual purpose spring/quivers by permitting the tip to be pushed back inside the spring. The idea behind the spring/quiver is that you fish with the quiver until the fish become cagey. Then you pull the indicator out of its housing to bring the spring into play. This collapses at the slightest indication of a bite and gives much greater sensitivity without the need to break down the tackle and start all over again.

Avoid using too soft a quivertip because this defeats the object of the spring. If the quivertip section bends more than an inch before the spring begins to lean over, you're still quivertipping!

Springtips come into their own on hard venues with little or no flow where you expect finicky bites. The rod is positioned

Above left: Simple bobbin indicator — still effective in calm conditions on stillwaters.

Above right: Rod positions when using a quivertip on flowing water.

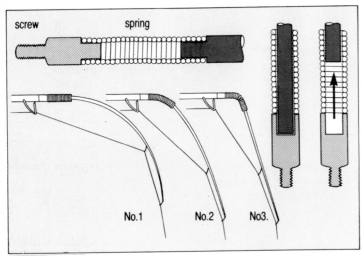

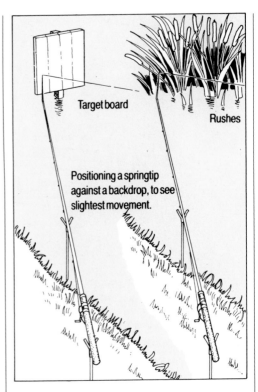

Positioning a springtip against a backdrop, to see slightest movement.

Target board

Rushes

Springtip

Above: 1. Tip too soft and is bending before spring. **2.** Tip bending slightly in unison with the spring. **3.** Tip bending before spring is effected. If you are buying a springtip go for type 3 action. With a dual purpose spring/quiver you'll probably have to settle for action 2. With action 1 you might as well be fishing with a quivertip, here the spring is only cosmetic. **A. Quivertip.** Tip pushed home in the housing **B. Springtip.** Tip detached from housing.

low so the line leaves the springtip at as near an angle of 45 degrees as possible. Spotting bites is made much easier if the tip shows up well against the background. Bear that in mind when setting up the rod or use a target board.

Springtips register tiny indications which wouldn't be revealed on a conventional quiver and that makes the background an important consideration. With this method the terminal tackle must be free running enough not to cause any resistance before the springtip is actioned. And tighten up the line slightly once the tackle has settled so the tip moves round about a couple of centimetres. That way it will register any drop-back bites.

Butt indicators

A butt indicator offers all the benefits of

a swingtip if you use it properly. The only disadvantage compared with a bite indicator fixed at the other end of the rod is that fractionally more resistance is set up with the line running through the rings before signalling a take. But this is useless if conditions are so bad that the swingtip sways continually at the rod end.

The length of a butt indicator is between 15 centimetres (6in) and 30 centimetres (1ft) but reckon on 24 centimetres (9in) as being the happy medium. Anything beyond 30 centimetres (1ft) will impede the cast.

Butt indicators are positioned on the rod with a Terry clip. The most suitable spot is midway between the reel and the first rod ring with the indicator leaning away from the angler. On some rods, the butt ring may be badly sited too close to the reel. If this is the case, a short 15 centimetre (6in) indicator may work better fitted above it and before the first intermediate ring.

After casting out with a butt indicator, the rod is placed in two rests pointing towards the end rig. The tip of the rod is submerged a few centimetres under the surface of the water to avoid excess movement on the indicator and rod tip.

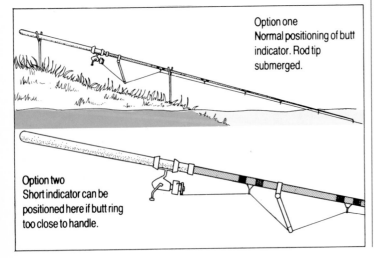

Option one
Normal positioning of butt indicator. Rod tip submerged.

Option two
Short indicator can be positioned here if butt ring too close to handle.

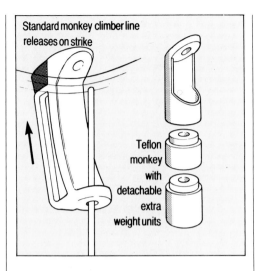

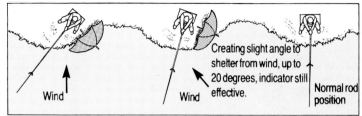

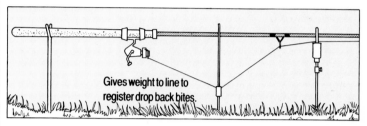

Once the tackle has settled the line is tightened up and then a little slack is given until the indicator is at an angle of just less than 45 degrees to the rod with the eye pointing upwards. This positioning allows for dropback registration which is common with this type of fishing. If weather conditions are atrocious, it is possible to position the rod at a slight angle to the end tackle — the butt indicator will remain reasonably effective.

Monkey-climbers

The most basic bite indicator for legering is a dough-bobbin moulded from bread and pinched on the line between reel and butt ring. It hangs with sufficient play to move upwards if a fish takes the bait and runs, or drops back down if the fish heads towards the rod.

There are more sophisticated versions of the dough-bobbin made from plastic or the much more stable monkey-climber type which is used on its own or with an electronic alarm as a visual indication of how a take is developing. The monkey-climb is a steel rod or needle between 45 centimetres (18in) and 90 centimetres (36in) in length on which the plastic indicator is free running.

Its advantages over a dough bobbin are that it disengages on the strike every time, something you can't guarantee with bread which has a habit of jamming in the butt ring. And it is stable in wind. Some needles are Teflon coated to prevent

Top : Rod positions in bad conditions.

Above middle: The monkey climber can be used on its own or with an alarm.

Above: The classic carp set-up of buzzer bars and monkey climber indicators. Note the stabiliser fitted to the rear bank stick which eliminates wobble in high winds.

Left: Flip-top indicator on the needle prevents any possibility of the line becoming tangled on a fast take.

Optonic bite alarm: the No.1 seller in carp fishing.

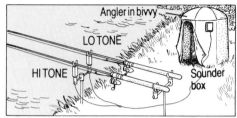

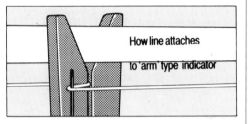

using extension leads.

Other electronic indicators include those which rely on the line being run behind an upright arm which is usually adjustable to combat drag. Once the line tightens against the arm as the result of a bite it sets off the alarm.

A compact little unit in the budget price range is the Aiken Sensotronic which is adjustable for different line diameters and has the option of light and sound detection. The Sensotronic doesn't have an arm and depends on the line pulling out from the jaws in the head.

Line clips

As with any form of bite indicator, deteriorating weather can cause problems with electronic alarms and it's wise to carry line clips or something similar to prevent false indications. There are two types of clip.

sticking and make the indicator extremely free-running. Most indicator bodies are now weight adjustable with take-apart chambers or sections and will accept an integral Betalight or small Starlight for nightfishing.

The monkey-climber is used for specialist forms of fishing on stillwaters and applies mainly to carp, tench and bream where long hours and possibly few takes are the norm. It's impossible to study a white plastic indicator for days on end and to ease the strain the majority of big fish anglers incorporate an electronic alarm into their set-up. This means they can study the water for signs of activity and relax behind their rods.

Optonic alarms with compact heads that allow the volume to be adjusted have become extremely popular. On the other hand you can opt for sensor heads which connect to a sounder box. This is positioned away from the rods, if required,

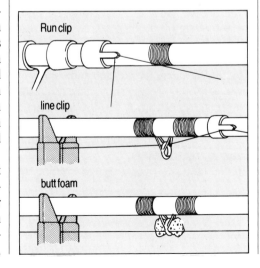

One is fixed on the rod in front of the indicator to prevent drag creating a false alarm. The other is known as a run clip and is taped to the rod handle directly above the spool of the reel.

When fishing with an open bale arm, line is trapped under the run clip to stop it peeling from the reel. Then there are pads of butt foam for inserting in the butt ring. Again, these prevent line running out until a proper run develops. They don't hinder playing of the fish.

The right rod

The ideal length for a feeder/quivertip rod is 11ft. This will punch out a loaded feeder and more importantly pick up line quickly on the strike to set the hook. Leger rods of 10ft are usually designed for fishing between 20 and 50 metres out from the bank. Most happily accept a light feeder as well as normal straight leger rigs.

The majority of carbon designs have medium actions and fine lines can be used safely for shy species like bream and big roach.

Wands of 7ft or less are restricted by their length for fishing inside the 20 metres boundary. But they're handy on windy days as the quivertip can be sheltered from the elements under a brolly to help spot bites. On canals, particularly, a short leger rod makes it easier to cast a light rig with inch perfect precision against far bank cover.

Although 12ft and 13ft beginner's rods tend to be equipped with a threaded top eye to take quivers or swingtips, these rods are too soft to cast any distance. Their very length also makes it tough spotting tiny bites at the rod end. A 7 to 9ft rod should be restricted to fishing distances up to 30 metres with a quivertip. After that 10 to 11ft rods should cover most eventualities up to 60 metres. Obviously, a more rigid blank is needed once the fishing distance increases. Custom-made rods of 12ft are suited to ranges beyond 60 metres but these are very fast tapered compared to match rods.

The specimen angler requires more robust rods to deal with long range casting

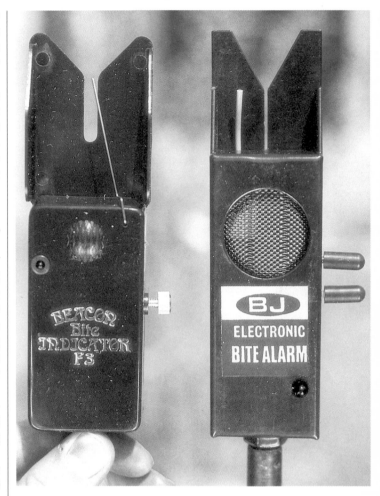

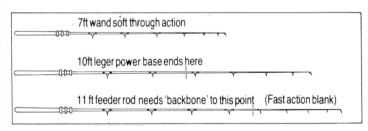

7ft wand soft through action

10ft leger power base ends here

11 ft feeder rod needs 'backbone' to this point (Fast action blank)

and bigger fish. Generally, 11ft is a good length to consider for fishing up to 60 or 70 metres, graduating to 12ft blanks for anything beyond. Specimen blanks are plain blanks without any form of spliced-in quivertips since they will be relying on electronic arms and monkey climb systems for bite indication. Test curves range from 1. 25lb up to 3.5lb, usually depending on the power needed for particular fish or distances.

Carbon and kevlar blanks are the front runners in this department. There are many actions from fast tapers designed for distance work to softer through-

Top: Arm-type indicators. Reasonably priced bite indicators which fall into this category include the Magno which can be adjusted to combat drag.The Beacon and BJ models shown above are also in the economy range.

actions for fish like tench and small carp at shorter range. It all depends on the individual's specific requirements. Most specimen rods are fitted with ceramic guides which are excellent and hard wearing. The one-legged models are very good on through-actioned rods as they don't affect the blank's action. There is also a trend with reel fittings to fit the screw-up types which hold the reel more securely for long casting purposes.

The right reel

A fixed spool reel for floatfishing which

A plastic leger stop and sliding bead carrying a non-toxic bomb — just one of many possibilities.

has a spare deeper spool will probably adapt pretty well for straight legering and light to medium swimfeeder work if you pack out the spool with 3 to 4lb line. But it will not stand up to the strain of heavy feeders. A light, specimen type reel is better suited to line of 4 to 6 lb because it offers a good retrieve ratio and a big diameter spool to help eliminate excessive line twist.

The chief reason for stepping up from a match reel to a specimen model for long range work is durability. A reel which has been designed primarily for fine lines may not absorb the punishment of repeatedly recovering heavier lines and weights from long distances or against stiff currents. Internal gearing wears very quickly on a reel that is not intended for long casting and there's always the threat of the bale arm mechanism opening up when overloaded.

Line

There is a good case for using prestretched line when legering because the lack of elasticity gives a more immediate pick-up from rod tip to hook on the strike. This also means the rod does not have to be swept through such a wide arc to set the hook. Prestretched, low diameter lines that team well with the straight leger include Drennan Double Strength and Ultima. But avoid using low diameter brands with the swimfeeder because they wear too quickly and won't absorb the shock of strenuous casting. Instead, select a more robust line like Maxima, Bayer Perlon and Drennan Specimen all off which rate as good feeder reel lines when breaking strains of 3 to 6lb are required.

Putting it all together

As with floatfishing, the reel spool must be filled to the lip for maximum casting performance. If a quiver or swingtip is fitted, check that it is aligned with the rod before threading the line through the rings. Then pull several yards off the reel and place the rod in its rests to sort out the end tackle.

First, the feeder or leger weight is slipped on the reel line followed by a small

London barbel specialist Ray Walton with a fish from the famous Pipes swim on the Hampshire Avon's Royalty Fishery at Christchurch. Ray nearly always legers a big chunk of meat and has taken many hundreds of specimens like this.

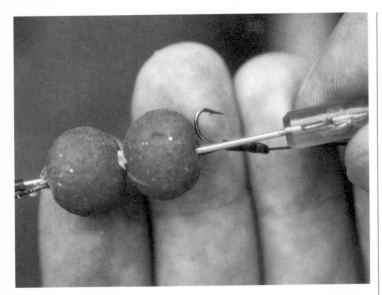

How to mount a boilie on a hair-rig.

Top: This is a Dacron hook link extended to form a hair with a Nash stop. The baiting needle has a blunt tip and fits into the concave end of the hair stop. Push the stop through the boilie as shown. In this case two baits are being used to prevent tench pouncing before the target carp.
Below: Remove the stop and withdraw the needle from the bait.

bomb to the end of the reel line. Cast out a few times and make slow retrieves and you'll soon pinpoint any snags. It could save valuable tackle.

River rigs

The open-end feeder, blockend and straight leger weight all have their days on river venues. A free-running American swivel link is fine for close-in fishing with a small feeder or Arlesey bomb. The swivel is stopped by a plastic leger stop or small split-shot — a number 6 to 8 is normally adequate — with a small bead as buffer. Always ensure the stop is positioned above the hooklength to avoid losing the feeder if you become snagged in some way.

Where the bottom is weedy or rocky, a simplified paternoster rig helps cut down tackle losses. It is easier to pull free if the bomb or feeder becomes trapped.

A stop-shot often proves a hindrance for long range river fishing as it collects bottom debris or floating weed. This can clog the swivel. Stop-shots are also likely to slip when retrieving tackle through strong currents.

A superior assembly that does away with any form of stop-shot is the loop system which works superbly for open-end feeders and also meets blockend and straight legering needs.

The loop is tied at the end of the reel line leaving an American snap swivel running free within its confines. The size of the loop can be varied but 45 centimetres (18in) is fine. At the bottom of the big loop, a much smaller loop is formed to which the hooklength is attached — it's crucial that this is formed exactly at the bottom and not slightly to one side or the rig won't hang correctly.

When cast out, the feeder rests at the base of the large loop with its weight pushing the hooklength out of the way to one side. Tangles are virtually non-existent on the cast and there's nothing on which underwater rubbish can collect. Anything that fouls the reel line comes to rest on the knot at the top of the big loop, well away from the main end rig. That loop gives

bead to act as a buffer against the stop shot or leger stop which goes on next. Leave just enough line to knot up an 45 centimetres (18in) hooklength and tie on the hook. Snip off any excess bits of nylon protruding from the knots.

Finally, rearrange the stop-shot or leger stop if you wish to move it closer to the hook or further away. Make a habit of baiting up the hook **BEFORE** loading the feeder. If you do it the other way around then mobile baits like maggots will have more time to wriggle free from the feeder before it is doing its job in the water.

Incidentally, it's helpful to search out the swim before tying on the terminal tackle. The easiest way is to attach an Arlesey

enough play for a fish to register bites on the quivertip. A fish would have to pull the tip right round before the feeder hits against the top of the loop, so no extra resistance is felt.

Lake rigs

The Arlesey bomb is the first choice weight for swingtipping. Its streamlined shape casts well and doesn't put too much strain on this ungainly looking bite indicator when it's hanging loosely from the rod tip on the cast.

Swimfeeders are also used in lakes and bream anglers prefer the open-ended model for introducing groundbait. A swim is normally topped up with the feeder and then the bomb is brought in when the bites start flowing. A rig similar to the river set-up with a stop-shot, bead and swivel is used but again it can be defeated by weed.

The paternoster is the best answer for minimal weed but thick growth which reaches a foot or so off the bottom calls for a modification.

Try switching the rig around so the bomb is at the bottom and the hooklength comes off the reel line, several feet back towards the rod. Then the hookbait is left suspended above the weed and in full view of the fish.

It is also possible to adapt the paternoster system to swimfeeders in weedy water and you can take this a step further by having a running link to the feeder.

With normal legering rigs and conventional baits, there are many permutations that can be made to induce bites like scaling down of the tackle in line strength and hook size. Specimen anglers cannot do this because of their powerful rods. This restriction brought about the development of the incredibly successful hair-rig.

The hair is a very short length of fine nylon or Dacron tied to the eye or bend of the hook. The hookbait is threaded on to the hair with a baiting needle and rests on a tiny plastic stop to keep it in place. Shy fish confidently pick up a hair-rigged bait because they cannot feel the weight

of the hook — it acts in the water just like a free offering. Once the bait is sucked inside the mouth, the hook follows and you're in business!

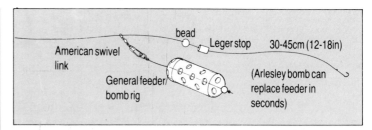

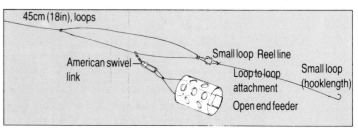

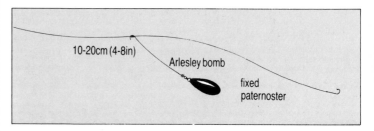

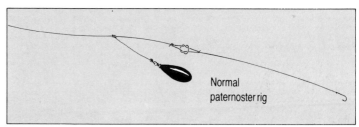

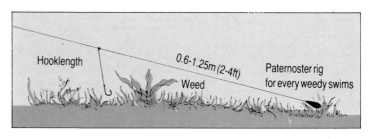

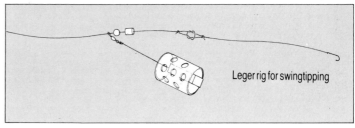

Popular river and lake legering.

ON THE LAKE

Let's imagine you've got the gear to make your fishing debut on a lake and look at what could happen in a typical session. The local tackle shop tell you the best catches are coming from the west bank of the water which is closest to the access point. That's not surprising as conveniently close swims tend to get most attention and with bait going in on a very regular basis the fish are inclined to shoal up in the vicinity. Walking round the west bank with your new tackle, the most likely looking pitch appears to be a well worn strip of bank facing an island. There are trees on the island which cast a deep shadow several metres out. The water looks dark and deep in this area and with a bright sun overhead the chances are that fish will be sheltering in the shadows alongside the island.

Another feature of the swim is a thick bed of weed immediately to your right stretching out from a bush. A good sized fish moves under the weed humping its back out of the water as you drop your tackle. It may even have been your silhouette against the skyline that startled it from basking at the edge. Several anglers are fishing open water swims and they've reported little sign of fish movement in the sunny, almost windless conditions.

A tilt device for precise positioning of the keepnet.

Net to the side

The tackle box is placed as near to the water's edge as possible on the sloping bank. The first job is to square up the box for a comfortable sitting position by withdrawing the extendable legs fitted to the front of the box by a notch or two. Next, the keepnet is staked out parallel to the bank in reasonably deep water which will give any fish you catch adequate freedom of movement. There's a temptation to sling it straight out in front but do this and you will be creating a snag for later on if a good fish is hooked and decides to dive into the meshing. The top ring of the net is screwed to a tilt device fitted to a bank stick. The stick is pushed vertically into the soft mud at your feet and the tilt mechanism fixed at the right angle so the net mouth lies horizontal to the water. A small point but it means you'll be able to slip fish into the keepnet from a sitting position.

The forward rod rest is attached to a long bank stick which extends out over the water. The shorter but adjustable back rest goes in vertically for stability as this bears most of the weight from the rod and reel. Take time to get it right because you don't want to be stretching out for the rod all day —•it needs to be the right height and within comfortable reach. A legering rod-rest with spaced slots for moving the position of the rod is left up the bank for the time being as the leger rig will only be called up if the float fails.

Because the bank is sloping it's going to be difficult to lay out a groundbait bowl and several bait boxes. Luckily, you've brought a bait waiter. This large, flat tray screws on a short bank stick and gives a stable horizontal surface on which to keep hookbaits, loose feed and groundbait.

The landing net is next on the agenda. It has a three-piece telescopic handle made from lightweight fibre glass and a pan-shaped net with a fine micro-mesh. The handle is 9ft long when fully extended — handy for reaching out over marginal weed. The mesh is soft and kind on fish and it's surprising how big a specimen will fit inside the pan design. A 20in diameter net swallows bream to 6lb with room to spare. The landing net is always made up before starting fishing — it's too late to fumble when a big fish is on.

During the session, any smaller items of tackle that may be needed are stored in the top sections of the tackle box which is a Continental type with pull-out trays.

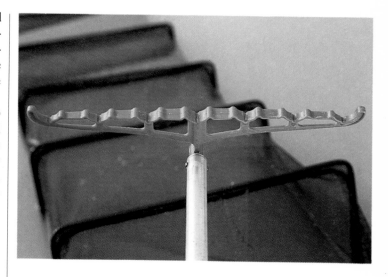

Putty plummet

Two float rods are made up. One is a powerful 13ft model for punching out a large waggler and the other 12ft to carry a light float rig, again fixed bottom end only, to explore the nearside swim.

First, the 13ft rod is used to plumb-up the depth against the island. It's quite a long cast and the customary plummet is too heavy for the job. Instead, a small piece of Sandvik malleable tungsten putty

Drennan rod-rest head gives the opportunity to fish a wide arc of water without repositioning the bank stick.

A pan-type landing net with soft mesh which is gentle on the fish.

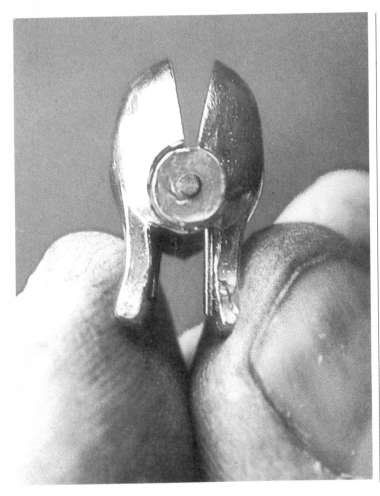

is pinched around the hook to overload the rig. The depth is guessed at two metres and the float set accordingly for the exploratory cast on the edge of the shaded water where it cocks then sinks out of sight. Obviously the float hasn't been set deep enough so it is moved up another foot and that does the trick. On the next trial cast the float tip just remains visible which indicates the hook is resting on the bottom — the ideal place to present the bait when starting a stillwater session. A few more exploratory casts are now necessary to gain a mental picture of the bottom right across the swim.

A slightly longer cast sends the float right under the overhanging branches against the island. The float only partly cocks which tells you the dropper shot are resting on the bottom as well as the makeshift putty plummet. As the highest of the dropper shot is 1.25 metres (4ft) from the hook, the tackle is edged forward to find the ledge where the water deepens.

Pulling the tackle in a couple of feet, the float sinks lower but still doesn't cock properly. This means there's only about a metre and a quarter (4ft) of water. Another slow retrieve over half a metre and the float sinks to its proper setting once

The most popular plummet design with spring-action jaws.

Right: How to plumb the depth with a waggler rig when fishing a feature like an island.
1 The first cast shows the depth is under 1.25m (4ft) because both dropper shot and plummet fail to register on the float.
2 The float sinks lower but one shot is still on the bottom as the depth is about 1.25m (4ft).
3 The float cocks correctly. Both drop shot must be off the bottom — leaving just the plummet touching.
4 The float sinks and, as the rig is set at 2.1m (7ft), the depth is obviously falling away.

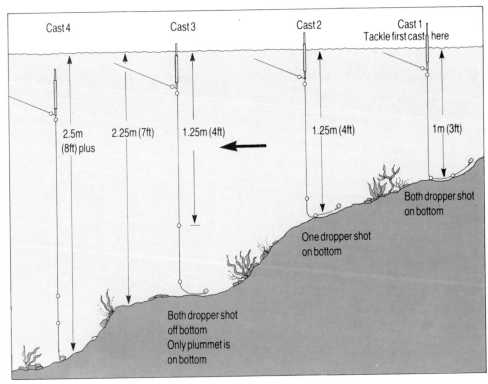

Cast 4   Cast 3   Cast 2   Cast 1
Tackle first cast here

2.5m (8ft) plus   2.25m (7ft)   1.25m (4ft)   1.25m (4ft)   1m (3ft)

Both dropper shot on bottom

One dropper shot on bottom

Both dropper shot off bottom
Only plummet is on bottom

the line is slackened off. This is the bottom of the shelf and about the point where the first trial cast was made. This is where the loose feed or groundbait needs to be introduced. But first the water needs mapping out from this spot right across to the nearside bank just in case anything else of interest is revealed.

Further exploration suggests the bottom evens out at two metres over a couple of metres then dips down into an open water gully, only beginning to shelve back up some 10 metres from the bank. This deeper water is less likely to hold many fish in mid-summer. But it's nice to know it's there because the fish will definitely spend some time in the gully during winter.

Extra time spent with the plummet is never wasted. It will often reveal fish-holding features like sunken weed beds and depressions. So after getting a feel for the outside swim, the other rod is picked up to investigate the inside line. This time a proper plummet is attached to the rig. This is because there's a nearside weed bed and it's possible that the small, light-weight piece of tungsten putty could give a false reading by resting on top of any underwater weed. Clip-on plummets are the easiest to use — they simply clamp over the hook.

Clean bottom

The bottom appears pretty clean up to the edge of the surface weed where there's a metre and a half of water. This is determined by pulling the plummet along the bottom to check if it gathers up any loose strands of weed. A couple of casts further out confirm that the water gets progressively deeper but with such a favourable depth against the weed it would be inexcusable to ignore this cover.

The baits you've been advised to bring are casters, hemp, squatts and a few big maggots to try on the hook. There's also a tub of small redworms in case the going gets tough.

Chief species in the lake are reputedly bream, tench, roach and crucian carp. There's also small perch and the chance

Mixing the groundbait.

Top: A little bit of everything they fancy! These are the base ingredients. Pour equal amounts of breadcrumb and the Continental groundbait of your choice into the dry mixing bowl. Thoroughly mix the dry ingredients. Dribble lake water into the bowl stirring vigourously until the correct consistency is achieved.

Middle: Mix in the hookbait sample.

Bottom: This consistency of groundbait is neither too stiff nor too soft.

of a mirror or common carp. With tench and bream in mind, two bags of Continental groundbait and a kilogram (2lb) of brown crumb to bulk it out will form part of your attack.

To start, you decide to feed groundbait on the inside line where there's more chance of finding a tench grubbing about in the weed and loose feed the island swim by catapulting casters. If there are fish in the shade of the trees, groundbait might spook them.

Half a bag of dark red Expo groundbait — a proven winner for tench — goes into the mixing bowl and an equal amount of breadcrumb is added. They're mixed dry before pouring in small amounts of lake water, stirring vigorously until the right consistency is achieved. The objective is to create a fluffy mix for the relatively shallow water.

When the groundbait feels right, two handfulls of casters are added with about the same quantity of freshly cooked

It's easy to cast a waggler accurately. Start with the correct grip, clasping the butt of the rod. Allow the rod tip to hang just past the vertical and line up on your target. A crisp punchy cast followed by careful feathering towards splashdown completes the sequence.

hemp. Finally, a few squatts are sprinkled in as tench seem to go for these. They'll also pull in the bream.

Four orange-sized balls of groundbait mix are moulded and lobbed in underarm alongside the weed-bed. They're not kneaded too firmly because they must break up quickly on the bottom. To try and attract the fish's attention even quicker, a few casters are scattered over the weed-bed. These loose offerings will filter down through the weed and if there are any fish below they'll start grubbing for them. That should lead them straight over the groundbait.

Now it's time to feed the edge of the tree cover by the island with a couple of cata-pult pouches of hemp followed by three good helpings of casters. A few casters are also fired right underneath the overhang-ing trees to draw out any fish towards the main feed area.

You start the session against the island because this is more likely to produce im-mediate results. The groundbaited area is left to settle. The 13ft rod carries 2. 5lb reel line with a two-swan insert waggler. There's a No. 5 shot three feet from the hook and an 8 dust midway between the two. The hooklength is 1.7lb tied to an 18 forged crystal design. You're not fish-ing too light at this stage in case there are any big fish about.

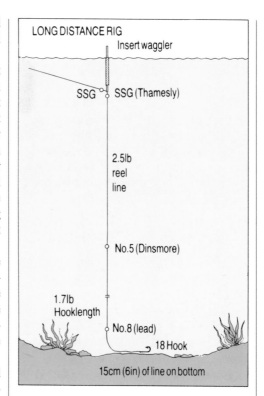

LONG DISTANCE RIG
Insert waggler
SSG SSG (Thamesly)
2.5lb reel line
No.5 (Dinsmore)
1.7lb Hooklength
No.8 (lead)
18 Hook
15cm (6in) of line on bottom

The tackle dealer advised against feed-ing big maggots as they attract hordes of small fry which are very active at this time of year. This doesn't prevent you from trying a couple of big red maggots on the hook. When feeding casters this is a good starting gambit and sure enough on the first cast the float dips under almost as it

Light groundbait 'pult. Upside down firing gives better accuracy.

Net at the ready.

Above: There comes a moment in any struggle with a sizable fish when you sense it's time to force the pace. That's when you should try and lift its head from the water on a tight line and start guiding it towards your net. Never chase the fish with the net. Keep it slightly below the water's surface at the point where you can trap the fish without over-reaching. It should all be unhurried.

Right: Immediately it's safely in the meshing, place the rod in the rest and grasp the landing net with both hands to withdraw.

settles. A steady, low sweep of the rod sets the hook and a 3oz perch is smartly reeled in.

A couple of fresh maggots go on the hook and a second cast is made just a metre or so further from where you want it to settle, and then drawn gently into position. Try to avoid dumping tackle directly on the spot you're fishing. If you overcast it is less likely to scare the fish congregating on the feed. The rig also settles more naturally.

Once the float is pulled into position, the rod is placed in the rests and about 20 casters catapulted around it. The rod is quickly picked up again as the No. 8 shot finally dots the float down. Regular loose feeding is essential to build the swim up and casters need to be introduced on every cast.

Better fish

There's no response after a couple of minutes so you try pulling the float in a few

centimetres. This almost sinks the float as the hooklength drags on the bottom but as the line is slackened off the insert tip lifts to its normal setting. A positive bite and another gentle, sweeping strike to the left puts a satisfying bend in the rod. A better fish this time. Injecting slight movement to the hookbait often attracts attention.

The fish boils just beneath the surface which means it is probably a skimmer bream as they tend to kite to the top very quickly after they're hooked. The rod tip is kept low, utilising its action to win line by easing it back by two or three yards at a time and then winding in as the rod is repositioned back out towards the fish to begin the same retrieve process again. Line is never wound back directly against the force of a better fish because the rod's action is negated and it could result in the hook tearing free or the line parting.

As the skimmer nears the rod, the tip is lifted higher and the fish brought to the surface. With your free hand, the landing net is submerged and the fish drawn over it. Never chase a fish with the net if it makes another dash for freedom at this critical stage. It will only redouble its efforts at escaping.

The skimmer bream scales about 1lb and is a light silvery colour, quite unlike more

How to play a fish.

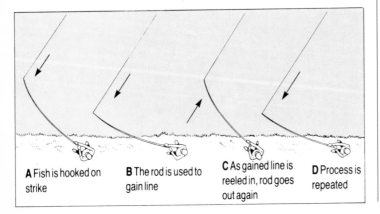

A Fish is hooked on strike

B The rod is used to gain line

C As gained line is reeled in, rod goes out again

D Process is repeated

Fish care and handling

Every angler shoulders the responsibility to protect fish stocks for future generations by unhooking and handling fish as humanely as possible.

If a fish has swallowed the hookbait, simply locate the slit at the head of the disgorger on the line and keeping the nylon taut, run it down into the fish's mouth. Once the disgorger hits against the bend of the hook it normally dislodges it automatically allowing it to be retrieved. Some times you may have to gently twist the disgorger around to find a better hold on the hook. But never use excessive force. If you can't free it, the fish has a much better chance of survival if you cut the line as close as possible to the hook.

Fish naturally pick up very sharp items like snail shells which are crunched up and passed through or regurgitated. In time, a hook will rust away. And if you use a barbless pattern the likelihood is that the fish will shed the hook quickly anyway.

The best possible contribution you can make to fish welfare is to handle them with extreme care for the shortest possible time. Indeed, it's often possible to virtually eliminate holding a fish out of water by unhooking a sizeable specimen in the confines of the landing net and transferring it in the mesh to the keepnet or releasing it immediately.

If you've got to handle a sizeable fish for a photograph, wet your hands beforehand then little if any of the protective mucous on the body will be removed. Never use a towel because it acts like sandpaper!

There are several ways of holding fish but the safest bet for the beginner is to support its head in one hand and to cradle the body towards the tail by the anal fin with the other.

If fish must be retained in keepnets, always ensure the net is staked out properly in water that's deep enough to give the fish plenty of movement. Never allow a keepnet to collapse and if possible position it in shade. The shallow margins can become very inhospitable on hot days. Also make sure your keepnet is big enough. It needs to be a minimum of 2m (6ft) in length with a diameter of 45 centimetres (18in) and must be knotless. Water Authority bye laws state minimum sizes — so check if in doubt or don't use a keepnet.

---

mature specimens which darken to bronze and almost black in some waters.

In the next 20 minutes, the maggot approach brings a small roach and two lightning-fast bites are missed. An 18 hook is hidden inside a caster and cast out towards the island followed by a sprinkling of loose feed. Nothing happens.

While you're pondering on the next step, it's as well to keep an eye on the nearside weed-bed for signs of fish movement. Clusters of tiny bubbles are the give-away that there's tench or bream down below feeding over the groundbait. For the moment, everything's quiet but another scattering of hemp and casters over the groundbait at regular intervals won't do any harm. Give it another half-hour before trying this and resist the temptation to top up with more groundbait until the swim has been given a try.

Dithering bite

Glancing back to the edge of the island, there's no sign of the float! A hurried strike results in a bumped fish. Another caster goes out and it's not long before a confident bite produces a nice 10oz roach. Then a double caster combination is tried and after a dithering sort of bite during which the float half submerges a couple of times, it finally sinks and a much better class of fish is securely hooked.

The fish's movements are ponderous which suggests it's probably a big bream

Casting up to weed

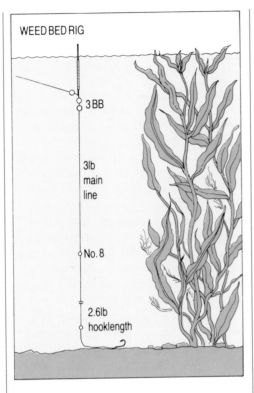

WEED BED RIG

3 BB

3lb main line

No. 8

2.6lb hooklength

you pulled in the float the rod tip was dipped below the surface of the water to sink the line.

As the float dots down a dozen casters are flicked around it with a smaller canal style catapult. Barely two minutes later there's a slight judder on the float tip followed by another. Then the float dips and you're in! The edge of the weed-bed boils but you can apply plenty of pressure against the fish with the softer actioned rod to stop it diving deep into the cover. The 1.7lb hooklength and forged hook with 3lb main line stands the strain and the fish is halted. It moves out into open water where it makes a couple of fast bursts. Clearly, this is no bream.

Gradually, a very dark shape nears the net but powers off just when you think it's going to submit and has to be carefully pumped all the way back again. A large, almost black head, tiny red eyes and thick-set body of a tench weighing about 2lb finally enters the pan net. That was close! The tackle just held out so before recasting the hook is changed to an eyed 16 made from heavier wire than the previous 18 spade end. The hooklength is upped to 2.6lb as when fishing against cover you can normally get away with heavier gear.

Buried in weed

The reason for changing hooks is that the spade-end can cut through the line with powerful fish like tench if they bore into weed. Another double caster offering brings a savage bite on-the-drop and a stubby crucian of 8oz is whisked out. Then you connect with another good tench and this proves unstoppable in its dash for the weed. The tackle goes solid but there is a suspicion the fish may still be attached.

Side-strain and direct overhead pressure fails to move the fish. Now the only option is to try giving slack line. That could trick the fish into thinking it is free and after a minute or so it might move out from its hiding place. You watch the line and it twitches a couple of times. Further pressure suggests the fish has dived even deeper into trouble. Just when everything looks lost, a large chunk of the weed

and sure enough after coaxing the fish in, using the rod to cushion any sudden movements, a large bronze flank shows on the surface. The fish is carefully steered over the landing net and once inside the rim, the net is lifted clear of the water. You place the rod in its rests to recover the landing net with two hands. Never lift a good fish like this or you'll snap fibre glass handles. It's about 2lb and is transferred to the keepnet with the minimum of fuss after carefully unhooking.

Another smaller bream follows then the swim suddenly dies. It's time to investigate the weed-bed at the nearside. The second rod is teamed with a waggler which takes 3BB locking shot with a couple of No. 8s down the line. This float has a longer, finer insert than the pattern on the other rod and the rig is set to fish 15 centimetres (6in) overdepth with the first No. 8 shot 15 centimetres (6in) off the bottom and the second a foot above that. Bubbles are bursting on the surface right by the weed. Nicely timed!

The second waggler rig is slightly overcast with double caster hookbait and wound in until it is almost touching the weed. There's a bit of a breeze now causing surface drift from right to left. But as breaks free and drifts towards you. Underneath there's a large, waving black tail! The landing net is dipped deep into the water under the weed and a careful lift engulfs the lot. You feel the fish hit against the side of the net and after disentangling it from the weed fronds it proves to be another tench.

The disturbance has ruined the inside swim and after a blank 20 minutes it is topped up with more groundbait and left alone again. It's back to the big waggler outfit and double caster on the hook in the shadow of the island and first cast produces a bream of 1lb.

The loose feed is still going in on every cast and the line needs to be sunk because that breeze is making control tricky.

The bites dry up and after changing the rig to fish even more overdepth you decide on a drastic change by shallowing up. Stepping up the loose feed produces a brace of skimmers hooked half a metre off the bottom and a 6oz roach but the swim seems to be dying fast.

One last possibility on this tackle is to cast very tight in to the island and beneath the overhanging trees. The float shoots away as a powerful fish grabs at least 15 metres of line and dashes away from the island. The fish slows down then charges off again on a zig-zagging run. This must be a carp by the feel of it and recovering line is a painfully slow exercise. Two minutes seem like 20 when you're playing a good fish but that's all it takes to net a 3lb mirror, not a big fish by specimen standards but a bonus on this gear.

The next hour sees little action and in desperation you scale down to a 1lb hook-length and fine wire hook. Result is two more bites from small roach.

Back on the nearside line there's no sign of tench but you try mixing a little more water into the groundbait to introduce a cloudier mix around the float on every cast. This appears to liven up the swim and a stream of small roach on maggot or caster hookbait are swung in with the odd skimmer to 6oz among them. A change to redworm earns a few tiny perch and a 12oz tench.

The session draws to a close and you've not done all that badly — nearly 20lb of fish

A pleasing morning's fishing on the Kingsbridge lakes in Dorset brought Dave Coster this mixed net that included some rod-thumping little mirrors

are released from the keepnet. But you're left with the feeling that the island swim held many more fish than your results suggested. The loose feed took rather a time to bring the better bream into the swim and it didn't hold them. Next time it will be worth considering groundbait, perhaps half-a-dozen big balls containing casters and squatts.

It also got more difficult later in the session to hold the big waggler on line in the face of the stiffening breeze. It might have been better to have switched to a swingtip or quiver.

As for the inside line, this underlined the fact that the lake holds plenty of small fish. The tackle shop reckoned the tench averaged 3 to 4lb but your fish were a lot smaller. Possibly the groundbait was responsible for attracting the smaller stuff and a bait like sweetcorn with loose feeding might have pulled a heftier fish.

Anyway, a sharp mental picture has been formed of the lake's potential by fishing the two lines and different methods of approach. The anglers who stuck it out in the open water had much less luck.

Then again, if it had been overcast it could have been a totally different story.

After that thought-provoking session on the lake described in chapter seven, your next challenge is a medium sized river about 20 metres wide with plenty of streamy glides over gravel and the odd deeper run between dense beds of weed. This imaginary fishery is renowned for barbel and contains specimen chub, dace and roach in considerable numbers. But today you're looking for plenty of bites on the stick float rather than singling out exceptional fish. This means less chance of a barbel because they've got a marked preference for a stationary bait nailed to the bottom.

The ideal swim needs to offer a decent trot downstream through all that weed. If it ends in deeper water, all the better, because that means there'll be an opportunity to draw fish up into your swim.

The fishery manager listens to your description of a perfect swim — and sends you on a long hike to the upstream boundary of his waters where there are extensive shallows bursting with weed growth. Then the channel constricts slightly forming two distinct runs which look full of promise. One is on the nearside some 10ft out offering a 20 metres trot between the weed. The other channel is near the far bank and glides smoothly below overhanging trees.

At the end of the swim there's a gravel bar which quickly plunges away into darker, deeper water. This swim should hold a lot of fish but it would be foolish to sit right on top of them. Far better to entice them up the nearside run where the stick float should handle well in the evenly paced water.

Marshy margins

The margins are rush lined and rather marshy which means you'll have to stand up to fish. But that's no bad thing with the stick float as it gives better control of the tackle.

The keepnet goes in first and it won't need staking out as the current quickly billows the mesh downstream. The rod rests are firmly fixed and the bait waiter follows with a longer bank-stick underneath to bring it up to your standing position. Many anglers prefer a bait apron in these type of swims but it does limit your choice as there are usually only a couple of pockets.

A pint of hemp goes on the waiter plus a similar quantity of casters, bronze maggots with a sprinkling of dark reds and a small bowl of very dry, cloudy groundbait. There's another pint of maggots in reserve and an extra half pint of casters — just in case the fish want a lot of feed. Another useful bait kept in reserve is a small bag of cooked tares. This bait works well with hemp when there's lots of small fish as it often sorts out the better samples.

The landing net is made up and placed near to hand leaving just the 13ft float rod to assemble with a closed face reel which will give a cleaner pick up and better line control than a fixed spool. The reel line is a supple, floating brand rated at 2lb.

The inside run looks as though it's going to be just over a metre deep and in smooth water like this the end tackle won't need to be all that weighty. A lignum stick is selected carrying four No.5 shot spread out between float and hooklength, tapering down to a No.8 then a 10 nearest the hook. The hooklength is a 1.7lb line ending in an 18 barbless Drennan fine wire hook. The wire in this particular pattern is strong enough to team satisfactorily with the hooklength.

For once, you've ignored plumbing the depth. A visual survey of the swim gives a good impression of what to expect and a rigorous plumbing exercise might spook fish already in the glide. To start, the rig is set at 4ft for a couple of test run throughs with caster. A hook completely hidden inside the shell of a caster is less likely to snag any unseen obstructions, unlike a maggot which is certain to catch up with the hookpoint fully exposed.

A helping of hemp and casters will be trickled into the swim on every other cast allowing the tackle to push through with the feed. The first couple of casts see the float travel the whole length of the swim unhindered so you try deepening off by 15 centimetres (6in). This causes the float to drag under two thirds of the way down. By holding the tackle back slightly once it reaches this spot and then letting it run, it's possible to trip the hookbait over the obstacle which is almost certainly a clump of weed. To confirm the depth, the float is pushed further up the line but it immediately drags under at the start of the trot. The tackle is reset at 1.5m (4.5ft).

Stopping the splash

The fifth trot of the session brings a fast bite just before the float needed to be held back to run over the underwater snag. A gentle upstream strike sets the hook and the rod arcs into a fair-sized fish. The tip is kept down near the water to prevent the fish from rising too high in the swim. If you lift the rod in shallow, flowing water

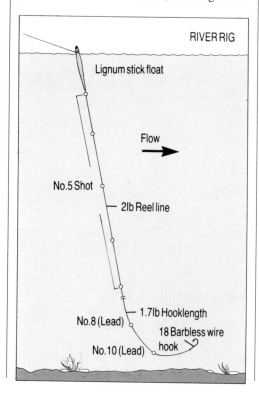

RIVER RIG

Lignum stick float

Flow →

No.5 Shot

2lb Reel line

1.7lb Hooklength

No.8 (Lead)

18 Barbless wire hook

No.10 (Lead)

then hooked fish will tend to splash on the surface and scatter the rest of the shoal.

The fish is carefully pulled up to the head of the swim by drawing it through the water with the rod flexed in an upstream direction. The pressure is then slightly eased as the rod is returned to its original position and that just gives you the time to recover some line. The net head is submerged and a lively 12oz chub flaps to the disgorger. The next 15 minutes produces two more chub from the same mould and some missed bites. All the action is materialising just before the snag but it tails away abruptly which leaves you pondering on your next move.

Cloud of attraction

The feed rate is stepped up but that doesn't bring any response. Then some small balls of cloudy groundbait are lobbed in on the next few casts in an effort to liven the swim. No fancy mixes are needed for this type of fishing. The groundbait is being used solely as a visual attractor and is a 50/50 mix of brown crumb and Super Cup which achieves a good cloud effect.

The groundbait draws back the fish and

Above: Under arm cast with the stick is performed with slow deliberation. The baited hook is gripped in the left hand with the rod held parallel to the river. Then swing the rod upwards and out over the river, swivelling the body to face the swim and releasing the bait simultaneously. In effect the rod sweeps through a 90 degrees angle and sends the tackle shooting out in a straight line immediately in front of your fishing position. The hookbait and shot should precede the float in a trajectory so the tackle drops in a straight line on the surface of the water. If necessary, feather the line slightly to ensure the stick follows behind the baited hook and strikes the water last of all.

Make a habit of loose feeding every other cast. The amount you introduce depends on the season and the reaction of the fish but let it dry up altogether and you'll considerably reduce your chances.

Opposite page.
Playing and landing.
Top: The current and solidly rooted weed make playing a sizeable river fish more evenly-matched on light tackle.

 Ease the fish towards your netting position by drawing it against the current on a light line and then dropping the rod tip slightly to release the pressure for a fraction of a second so the line can be recovered in stages.

Fish always find an extra burst of energy when they spot the net and that's the time when most losses occur. With less line between you and the fish and therefore reduced elasticity, greater strains (Continued on p. 95)

you return to loose feeding as some sizeable dace snatch at the bait on every trot. You almost have to anticipate the bites from these silvery little fish as they race in and out and give lightning fast bites. But you're helped by the fact that most of the bites are coming at roughly the same spot. That groundbait certainly got things moving but it won't be used again unless the bites dry up as it might hinder the chances of finding better chub.

All of a sudden you bounce the tackle out of a better fish. That's the sign to ignore the dace for a spell and deepen off the float by 30 centimetres (12in). Double caster goes on the hook and the tackle is cast slightly downstream for a change and held back hard. The hookbait is edged down to the taking spot, still on a tight line and the float pulls away sharply. It's a much heavier fish which slams the rod round and then judders the tip several times. This immediately tells you it's a good chub. These fish often shake their heads vigorously to try and dislodge the hook. The light tackle absorbs the pressure but it's touch and go as the fish tries to bore into the weed flanking the channel. Each time this happens, the rod is positioned low and in the opposite direction to which the fish is moving.

 The chub is finally coaxed to the top and once its head is above water, it is drawn over the waiting net. Never try to net chub while their head is still submerged—they'll dive right around it and possibly smash the line. This is a nice fish of nearly 3lb, a lovely bronze-sided specimen with a

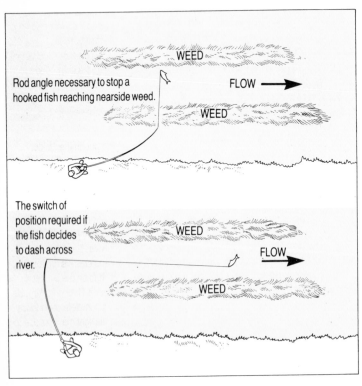

Rod angle necessary to stop a hooked fish reaching nearside weed.

WEED

FLOW →

WEED

The switch of position required if the fish decides to dash across river.

WEED

FLOW →

WEED

much broader head and huge mouth compared to the smaller dace. The double caster attracts no further interest but a single offering on the same tackle produces another head-shaking chub and a couple of smaller fish. The commotion of playing them out quietens the swim.

The loose feed is maintained and you try the different shotting patterns the stick float permits, picking up the odd bonus dace. But you're really having to work the tackle to tempt bites now.

As the hookbait tumbles through the top layer of water you notice a couple of fast knocks before the tackle rights itself. This suggests fish have moved right up top after the loose feed. The float is shallowed off slightly and following the usual under-arm cast it is held back immediately it hits the water. This slows its descent — but not enough it seems as a fast bite is missed. Two of the No. 5 shot are pushed up underneath the float and the remaining ones spread out. This time the float sinks away before it settles and a good dace results.

Two more missed bites encourage you to try double maggot as it's time consuming rebaiting with caster. A few more dace take the bait but there's not enough action to warrant a switch to loose fed maggots.

Tares turn them on!

The bites are coming right under the rod top now the fish have been drawn up the swim by the loose feed. There seems to be a sizeable shoal but they've grown shy of the caster. Possibly it's the hemp that's holding them. A single grain is carefully trapped on the hook and this brings a plump 12oz roach. Time to give tares a whirl!

Tares are much easier to use than hemp. They don't come off the hook so often on the strike and if you miss a fish or two are put on the tackle. At this stage of the fight, there's often a need to give a bit of line probably by backwinding rather than depending completely on the clutch. **Above:** Dave Coster completes his capture of a chub on the Dorset Stour's Throop fishery. He has complete confidence in his light match tackle to soak up pressure. But there is no real substitute for experience.

Big roach expert Owen Wentworth shows one of his many fine winter specimens taken long trotting in a swim that was choked with weed just a couple of months earlier.

there's no need to rebait every cast.

This bait change brings a flurry of roach and the feed is now confined to small helpings of hemp on every cast. Dace take a liking to the tares as well and another 2lb chub hits the net. Tares are not a bait you can drag overdepth in flowing water because they're heavy and catch up too easily. The only way to fish tares on the bottom is by holding back the tackle hard. You try this with the rig again set overdepth and catch another couple of roach.

The keepnet at your feet contains double-figures now and it's the moment to experiment with a complete change of tactics. The plan is to introduce a bed of hemp and maggots right under the rod top to see if it's possible to draw in a barbel. A bait dropper is the most accurate way of feeding fish in flowing water and a good half-dozen loadings of both hemp and maggots are spread in the swim.

This disturbance isn't going to do your chances any good for some time and you won't lose anything by retiring the stick float for a while to set up a quivertip rod.

It only takes a few minutes to rig up a light bomb to a 3lb reel line and 2lb hooklength. An 18 forged hook complements the rig and to begin with the bomb will be cast to the end of the previous float swim. You never know, there may be the odd fish lurking down there picking up loose particles of bait.

After the rests have been repositioned to take the quivertip rod, the first cast is placed just before the gravel bar at the end of the swim. More loose feed is introduced, this time further downstream.

A few casters are also flicked over the second run across at the far bank. There are almost certainly a few chub lying under the bushes.

The leger rig is baited with a maggot and caster cocktail and the rod positioned pointing straight out over the water. The sensitive quivertip rattles encouragingly as small dace bang away at the hookbait. Then the tip pulls round hard and you net the best roach of the session scaling 1lb. The rattling bites stop and the bait is flung across the far bank under the bushes. The rests must now be repositioned again to lift the rod tip higher so the line doesn't foul the midriver weed.

Hard pulls on the quivertip fail to develop into anything more positive and you suspect the fish are feeling the resistance of the tight line and dropping the bait. The answer is to release a little more line into the water after the next cast to form a slight bow. There's no missing the bite that follows as you've got much more time to react. A small chub followed by a two-pounder appears to be as much as you can expect from the far run and now it's time to fish a stationary bait under the rod top with the stick float rig held back well over-depth.

The float is pushed up by a couple of feet and the No. 5 shot grouped around the hooklength knot. A BB is added to this new bulk weighting to overshot the float and stop it from riding up. The hook also needs to be changed for a stronger, forged pattern with a couple of maggots attached.

To settle this rig properly, the tackle is swung out underarm as before but in a downstream direction and a tight line retrieved back up towards the rod tip. The rod can be positioned in rests for this more

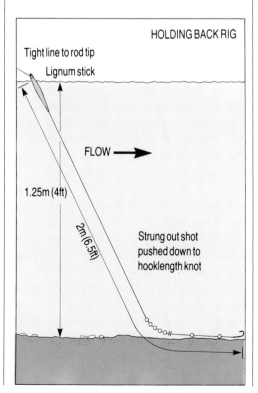

HOLDING BACK RIG

Tight line to rod tip

Lignum stick

FLOW →

1.25m (4ft)

2m (6.5ft)

Strung out shot pushed down to hooklength knot

leisurely form of laying on.

The float tends to rise up when held back hard as the current fluctuates but bites are usually pretty positive. The float has to be pushed further up the line before it rides satisfactorily and you're happy that the bait is hard on the bottom. You know that's the case because a gudgeon nips in and snatches the bait and you switch to three maggots to foil the little fish.

A long period of waiting saps your confidence but the float then dives under without warning. A gentle lift of the rod and the tip lurches over almost into the water. The reel's anti-reverse is flicked off and the clutch tightened down. You need to give line by backwinding on this fish - that way you'll have much better control.

The fish is now halfway down the swim and threatening to reach the underwater snag. You apply sidestrain using the full power of the rod and thankfully everything holds. This is too much for the fish and it slowly works its way upstream until

The bait dropper solves the problem of getting hookbait samples down deep in fast flowing water.

it hugs bottom under the rod. It is tiring fast under the relentless pressure. A long, streamlined fish flashes beneath the surface. It's a barbel OK and it makes a few final half-hearted lunges before sliding over the net rim. Throughout these closing seconds of the fight you've avoided making any hurried movements which could panic the fish and send it diving for the bottom.

Barbel breather

The barbel looks to be around 4lb and the hook is carefully withdrawn from its rubbery mouth using a pair of forceps. The fishery rules forbid keeping barbel in keepnets and it must be returned immediately with its head pointing upstream against the flow. Steadying it with both hands in the current, the fish soon recovers and a twist of its body indicates it's ready to swim off.

Barbel often exhaust themselves during the fight and need watching because they have a tendency to float belly up and could drift out of reach unless tended first in the margins. Your fish was by no means exhausted but it still needed a breather before recovering sufficiently to hold station against the current.

The barbel proves the climax of your first river session but the double-figure catch was only achieved by adapting your methods to suit the way the swim performed on the day. Sticking rigidly to one method or bait would have realised a much leaner return.

The secret of river fishing is to keep the tackle versatile and your mind active. Try and look ahead to what your next move is going to be if bites tail off. The fish can only move up or down the swim or further out. If you adapt your tackle accordingly you'll soon find them again.

But the river will not always be in perfect trim and many times you'll find the best swims already taken. If there's a lot of extra water surging through then you can forget about the hotspots anyway. It's very doubtful that the fish will remain in these swims during floods.

When the river level lifts you'll need to seek out slacks or steadier runs and don't be deterred if these are only to be found in normally unproductive areas. Flood water changes the river dramatically and turns the formbook upside down. Small irrigation channels and sidestreams are worth investigating and lack of depth is no deterrent. A good bag of fish can be taken from 12in. of water when coloured up by heavy rain.

Slacks can be explored with light float tackle - a light stick is fine or a small balsa if the water's boily. On the main river, fish often move very close to the bank in times of flood to shelter from the excessively strong currents. Laying-on can score in these swims using a similar rig to that which produced the barbel earlier. The leger or swimfeeder also plays its part in these conditions. Look to use these tactics when the float won't hold or keeps pulling under because of the surface boil. There will be lots of rubbish washing through the middle layers of water so it's best to leger downstream of the rod top then less of it will foul the line.

Fish leger tackle close to the edge if you can find slower water or search out slacks created by fallen trees or moored boats. You'll also find productive slacks behind

Where to find fish on a rain affected river
x   indicates likely fish holding spots

Flooded area

Irrigation channel   stream   Flow

Moored boats

Trees or bushes hanging in water

Slack inside bend

Ditch

Cattle drink

Slacker water by bank bridge

bridge buttresses and on the normally shallow water on the inside of sharp bends.

When the river is running at its usual pace but most of the likely looking swims have been taken by other anglers, there's still plenty of options open to you. Dace, chub and even barbel are often found in shallow water where a stick float rig wouldn't work. The dumpy little Trent Trotter float fits the bill perfectly in these swims and will ride through water as shallow as 6in. ! These fast shallows require loose feeding on every cast to keep the fish from dispersing once their numbers have been thinned out.

Thickly weeded or overgrown areas nearly always hold a good head of fish. Laying on with float gear on a tight line in gaps among the weed is particularly effective when a bait dropper is used. The other possibilities include rolling a light leger under overhanging cover.

Shallow cattle drinks are mostly ignored but roach, dace and chub nearly always seem to lie just downstream of these churned up banksides. Coloured water and dislodged food particles are the obvious incentives for them to stay put.

A final option on a crowded river bank is to leger into holes among the very weedy areas with the rod tip pointing skywards. The feeder is productive in these tight swims and strong tackle is obviously necessary to bully out the fish. Prop the rod in a single rest with the butt resting on your tackle box so it's immediately at hand. If the bites are very fast and violent then touch legering may prove the best tactic.

A tidy catch of chub, roach and dace taken on a light stick float rig at Throop in mid-summer.

ALL ABOUT THE POLE

Right: What to look for when choosing a pole.

Below: The pole applies direct overhead pressure on a fish giving much greater control. It means you can play out a big fish even in weed holes like this. Weed is festooned up the line and around the fish and Dave is finally forced to dig out his catch. The fish and weed together add up to a hefty netful.

Before setting out to chose a pole, you must know what you require of it. Basically, there are two reasons for using a pole. One is for uncluttered speed work, fishing a long line to hand. The other is for better presentation of your tackle — beyond the distance you can achieve with a rod and reel.

The crucial consideration when purchasing a pole is how long a model you require. If you fish small canals a great deal then 11 metres will put you tight up against the far bank. For lake fishing, ten or 11m is fine and the same goes for river work. Most pole fishing revolves around the 7 — 8 metre mark but it's useful to have the extra sections if the fish move out or a big one is hooked.

Pick the longest pole you can afford — that's the best advice. But it should feel responsive and not sloppy when fully ex-

tended. It should not sag unduly either although all poles droop to some extent beyond 8m. The trick is to pick the pole with a very gradual curve instead of models that sag at a pronounced point — usually this is the second joint from the butt. A pole that sags badly at your end will transmit the sag down the pole on the strike resulting in bumped fish or crack-offs on fine hooklengths.

Ask your dealer about spare top sections. It can be very handy to duplicate the top three or four sections of any pole

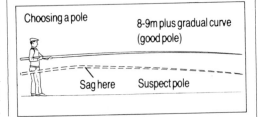

Choosing a pole

8-9m plus gradual curve (good pole)

Sag here   Suspect pole

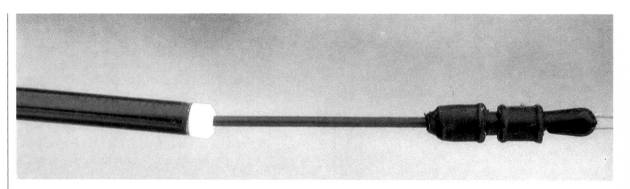

then you can have a couple of rigs made up on the bank for fishing two different lines of attack. If you can only stretch to a medium priced pole that is a little shorter than you think you really want, try and pick out a model which has optional extension pieces then you may be able to add to the pole's length at a later date.

Flick tip or elastic?

There are two ways of rigging out the top sections of a pole. The simplest method is to use a flick tip which is usually a spliced in piece of solid carbon about 45cm (18in) long to which the line is attached direct. This fine carbon or fibre glass tip can also be used as a shock absorber once a fish is hooked. But there are obvious limitations.

Most pole anglers use flick tips when after small fish with baits like breadpunch, squats and bloodworm. It is more immediate on the strike for hitting finicky bites.

But where larger fish are expected then it's wise to use the elastic shock absorber. The most favoured set-up is the internal system which entails threading the elastic through the top two sections of pole. For this you will need a hollow top section or you'll have to cut the flick tip back just below where it is spliced. A PTFE bush is then fitted into the end to allow the plastic a free, smooth running passage out when under tension.

For tangle-free fishing, most pole anglers attach the elastic to a Stonfo elastic/line adaptor which has a quick-change release facility so you can change over pole rigs in seconds. Most pole elastic is colour coded now and here's a guide to their breaking strains and usages.

Colour	Breaking strain	Hooklengths
White	12oz	5-10oz
Red	1lb	10-14oz
Green	1.25lb	12oz-1.1lb
Blue	2.25lb	1.1-1.7lb
Black	3lb	1.7-2.6lb
Yellow	4lb	2.6-3.2lb

Handling methods

It's not easy to fish with 12m of pole even if you've got a very light model. Far better to learn how to handle 7 or 8m first and to restrict yourself to small fish for an apprenticeship period. Start on a canal or lake with plenty of small roach and skimmer bream and fish for them with fine tackle and small baits like squatts or breadpunch. Several hours spent knocking out 50 or 60 small fish will be invaluable. You'll soon get the knack of how to unship several sections of pole at once without jolting a small fish off the hook.

More importantly, you'll appreciate the improved tackle control this method provides. Leave the bigger fish alone and the extra sections on the bank until you've mastered fishing up to 8m — which is a comfortable distance to throw loose feed or groundbait.

Unshipping sections

The easiest way of unshipping the sections on a long pole is to use a pole roller or your rod holdall positioned a couple of

Quick-release clip fitted to internal elastic.

Flick tip and second section of pole fitted with internal elastic.

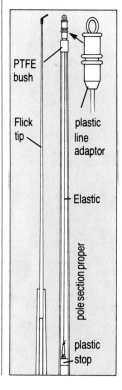

PTFE bush

Flick tip

plastic line adaptor

Elastic

pole section proper

plastic stop

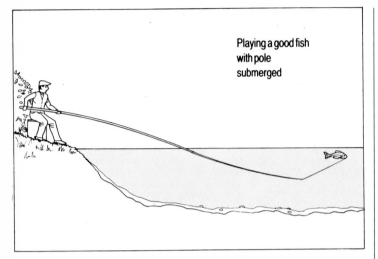

Playing a good fish
with pole
submerged

metres behind you and to slide several sections backwards at once. When using a flick tip or fine elastic shock absorber, the best way to bring the pole in, while unshipping sections, is to dip the top section under the water. This will cushion any jerky movement and helps to prevent bumping fish off the hook. This method works well for fish up to about 1lb.

Obviously, it is not always possible to bring the pole back directly behind you, especially on a narrow canal towpath. If the pole has to be brought round to the side while a fish is on, to unship sections

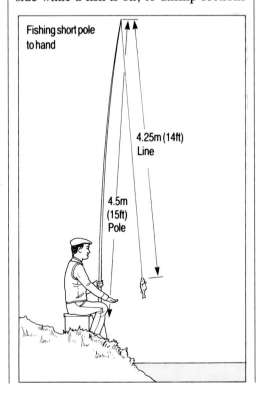

Fishing short pole
to hand

4.25m (14ft)
Line

4.5m
(15ft)
Pole

it is probably better to keep the tip just above the water and to let the top sections and the flick tip — or elastic system — absorb any rough movements.

The only time the pole should be kept high when landing a fish is if a big specimen has been hooked and the swim is snaggy on the nearside. In this situation try and get the fish to the surface or high in the water and then bring it towards you, taking off one or two sections at a time.

The trick when fishing for larger fish against far bank snags, is to sink the pole tip very deep in the water while it is being pulled in. This often prevents the hooked fish from boring into snags overhanging into the swim.

Short or long?

Perhaps the easiest method is fishing a short pole to hand. Matchmen often fish this way for speed purposes when there are a lot of small fish about. There are a variety of rigs you can use but the main criterion is that the end tackle can be swung in to hand without breaking down whatever length of pole you are using. Most anglers find this is best achieved with a rig which ends just short of the butt of the pole. This allows for the pole bending over when a fish is swung in.

The long pole comes into its own when spot-on presentation is needed to tempt shy biting fish. On running water you can slow a hookbait down against the flow or stop it dead at far greater range than a rod and reel would allow. For this type of fishing use a longish line between pole tip and float for greater flexibility, say 1.25 to 2m (4 to 6ft) On stillwaters, a much shorter line is often needed — 60 to 100cm (2 to 3ft) tightens up the control and speed at which you can lift into bites.

Another successful long pole method is fishing tight over to cover on small rivers and canals. Inevitably, the depth will be shallow so a very short rig is used with very little line between pole tip and float — sometimes it is as short as 30 centimetres (12in).

Weights and floats

The Olivette remains a firm favourite as a bulk weight for pole rigs. In the most popular sizes, it is now outlawed in lead but there are several good non-toxic designs. At the top end of the range are Streamline tungsten Olivettes which are heavier, size for size, than the lead weights they've replaced. These weights have a large central bore but the manufacturers supply silicone tubing which fits the hole exactly to act as a buffer.

The Lock and Slide range made from brass have no central hole but are fixed to the line top and bottom with silicone tubing. No stop shot are needed and they are easily moved over knots. A heavier or lighter weight can be attached in seconds without breaking down the rig.

The Trimstyle Olivette consists of coiled copper wire wound on to fine silicone tube and you can peel off small lengths of wire to adjust their weight. Trimstyle are stopped on line conventionally with a stop shot or the thinner inside core can be crushed with forceps to anchor them in position without damaging the line.

Styl-leads and micro-shot

For finer presentation, Styl-leads or micro-shot are called up. The reason for using Styl-leads on a hooklength instead of micro shot is quite simple. A string of these will give the hookbait a slower descent. This has been taken a step further with very small pole floats on which Styls are now fished all the way down the rig for on-the-drop presentation.

Styls can be irritatingly difficult to apply to fine lines or dead easy—it's your choice. Without the proper Styl pinchers you're wasting your time. Even if you do fix them on the line they'll never be stable. Many anglers are put off buying Styl pinchers because they look more clumsy than ordinary forceps or tweezers. But they are just right for the job. The Styl-lead dispenser has fenced off areas for each compartment to spill out its contents. The idea is that you select those Styls which tumble

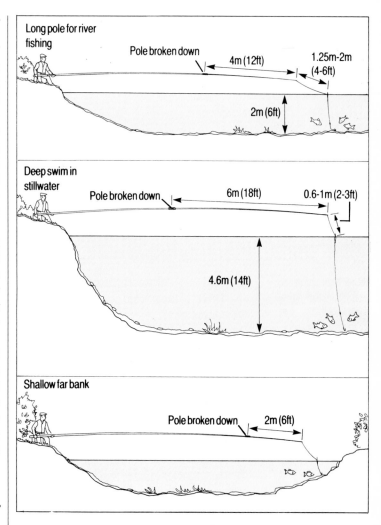

out face down by picking them up with the jaws of the pinchers and then nipping them on the line. The pinchers give an even pressure along the whole length of the Styl keeping the line dead central so it won't spring out at the ends when the line is taut.

Generally, micro shot are less tangle prone than Styls so use them when a lot of fish are expected. Styls come into their own when the fishing is hard. They give just a slight edge which can make all the difference when baits like squatts and bloodworm are used.

Float factors

When selecting a selection of pole floats certain questions must be asked to narrow down the choice. For example, you need to ask yourself which floats will benefit

Breaking down different lengths of pole for different fishing situations

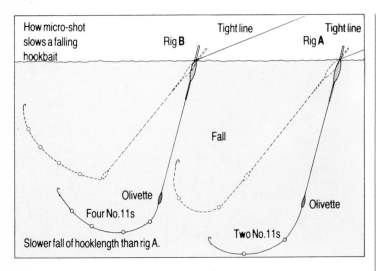

How micro-shot slows a falling hookbait

Tight line
Rig **B**

Tight line
Rig **A**

Fall

Olivette

Four No.11s

Olivette

Two No.11s

Slower fall of hooklength than rig A.

Above: How spreading more micro-shot slows a falling hookbait.

your fishing. Do the different designs really offer a functional advantage or are they gimmicky?

Some good looking floats are made to catch the angler's eye — but don't be misled into thinking an attractive cane stem is simply cosmetic or a wire stem purely for easy storage on a winder. Body shape is also important. Some bodied floats work better than others for river fishing, especially when holding back against heavy flow. In the same vein, slim shaped floats can out perform bodied designs in certain situations. Longer and bigger floats are also more suited for particular conditions.

Cane or wire stem?

Far right: Wire and cane stem pole floats with a choice of bodies.

Cane stems give a float better flight through the air when an Olivette is being

used and that's why they're recommended for fishing to hand. This can involve fishing a very small float with the same length of line as the pole being used for close in work, say two to five metres.

But it is also popular to fish much longer poles in the same manner for speed purposes. All this requires is to beef up the float size to get the tackle out. For five to seven metre lines use a No. 7 to 9 Olivette, eight to ten metres anything between a No. 10 to 15.

Wire stems are there purely to stabilise a float — to give the angler better control — and that's particularly welcome in blustery conditions. By losing some of a rig's weight in the float itself, it is possible to retain a high degree of sensitivity while retaining the correct weight loading to make a task like fishing a long pole a great deal easier.

The three chief styles of float can be broadly categorised as slims, body down floats and body up. There are varying degrees of sensitivity within each banding but the slims are the most delicate design and are chiefly used on canals and stillwaters.

The body down models take over when the slims become unstable in adverse conditions on canals or in deeper swims. The body ups are ideal for holding back in flow or ordinary trotting work.

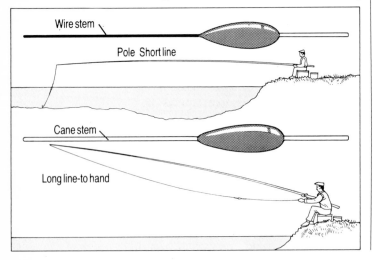

Wire stem

Pole Short line

Cane stem

Long line-to hand

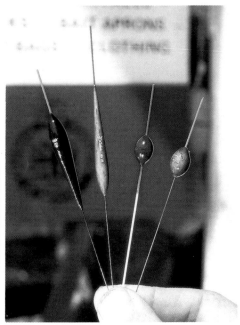

Surface float

There is still a shortage of good surface fishing floats and it is best to improvise your own designs out of peacock quill. For this type of fishing the float doesn't need to be fancy. It is purely on the line to add casting weight.

Once the float has landed on the surface of the water it can be ignored! It's far better to watch the hooklength line which should be crimped up with a fingernail for better visibility.

With this rig it helps to grease the hooklength for improved floatability and visibility. Bites are easily spotted — the coils of line snake away below the surface. With an extra long hooklength, a tiny number 13 shot can be added near the hook causing the coils of line to sink very slowly. Bites either move the float along the surface or speed up the line sinking dramatically.

Shotting patterns

Most pole floats are so sensitive that it takes quite a deal of time to set them up correctly. It's a difficult task on the bank and that's why it's a good idea to prepare them at home, storing a good selection of ready to use rigs on winders. The diagrams above will help get you started.

Rivers

A bulk weight is essential for the majority of river pole fishing. The easiest and least tangle prone is the Olivette. The best balance is achieved by weighting a float with an Olivette slightly lighter than the float's full capacity, leaving enough scope for the addition of two or three dust shot.

For this type of fishing a main line is used and a lighter hooklength. The Olivette is always positioned on the main line, never the hooklength. This avoids losing the bulk weight if the hook snags up. Usually, the hooklength is between 45 and 60cm (18 and 24in) long to gain sufficient elasticity from the lighter, more fragile line.

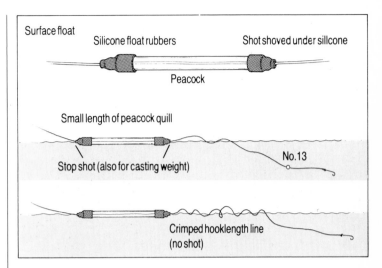

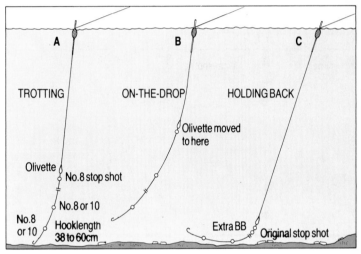

Shotting patterns.

But sometimes you'll find the hooklength needs to be shortened considerably when fishing small fish baits like bloodworm. Here the loss of some of the hooklength's shock resistance is overcome by using an elastic shock absorber.

For trotting work the Olivette is positioned just above an 45cm (18in) hooklength, stopping it with a No.8 shot with two No.8s or 10s at equal distances down the hooklength. In slow currents it can be helpful to use lighter Styl weights instead of dust shot to give an even slower rate of descent to the hookbait.

With this versatile river rig you have the option of moving the Olivette up the line as far as mid-depth to create a slow on-the-drop rig if the fish move up in the water. Or you can deepen the float and hold the tackle back hard against the flow to slow its rate of movement through the swim.

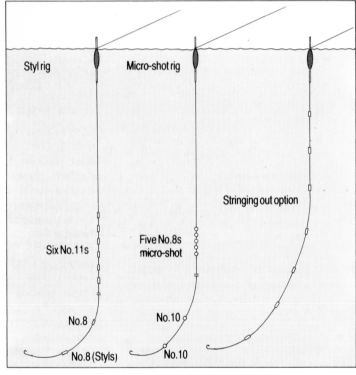

Styl rig   Micro-shot rig

Stringing out option

Six No.11s

Five No.8s
micro-shot

No.8

No.10

No.8 (Styls)   No.10

Top: Pincers for picking-up and fixing Styl-leads on the line.

Above: All Styl or micro-shot pole rigs.

With the second rig it usually helps to add an extra shot, something like a BB, below the Olivette. This is called over-shotting and prevents the float from riding up out of the water when you hold the tackle back or edge the float through the swim. It is probably the most tightly controlled form of pole fishing and on hard days you get bites you'd never have seen on conventional gear.

Canals

A much lighter variation of the river rig can be fished effectively on canals where the Olivette is often used for speed instead of control to get the hookbait down quickly among the fish when they are feeding energetically. It also helps plunge the bait through to quality fish down below without it being pinched by small fry up top.

When more finesse is required a string of micro shot or Styl-leads are used in preference to the Olivette. They can be strung out in normal stick float fashion or grouped as a bulk weight where the olivette would have been. The idea is to fish normally with this set-up until the fish move up in the water or become cagey. Then you experiment by stringing the weights out for a slower rate of descent.

Styl weights react very differently to a bulk weight. They can pick up subtle undertow and pull the tackle through more naturally, gaining vital extra bites on hard venues.

Lakes

Although the shape of float is likely to be different for lake or stillwater fishing, the weighting down the line can be very similar to river or canal rigs. In shallow water, the canal set-up is recommended while for deep water the river Olivette rig can prove useful in getting the hookbait down speedily or improving control over awkward surface drift.

Sometimes, a compromise of a high olivette and then a string of small Styl-leads down to the hook works wonders, especially for fish like skimmers and roach which tend to intercept a hook bait just as it settles.

Lines for the pole

Forget about the lines you use for free running rigs when you switch to the pole. Your favourite waggler or stick float line may not be supple enough to give proper presentation with delicate pole floats. If you're fishing an elastic shock absorber with the pole, then you can afford to use a much lighter breaking strain. It is also possible to incorporate much finer hook-lengths, down to as light as 5oz! If you're using very low breaking strain hook-lengths, the main line doesn't have to be quite as heavy as you're used to on running line. For example, lines from 5oz up to 12oz tied on the hook can be matched to 1 — 1.5lb main lines which will hardly affect a delicate pole float. The same float might react very differently with 2lb line which could pull it off course and even lift the float up out of the water.

So when you come to making your pole rigs up, what breaking strains do you base them on? Well, 12oz line is very fine and hard to break with internal elastic. The elastic puts 12oz into the category of 1.5

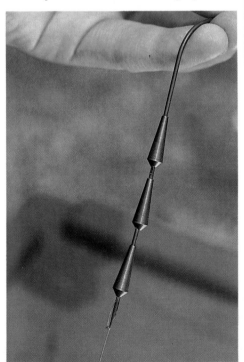

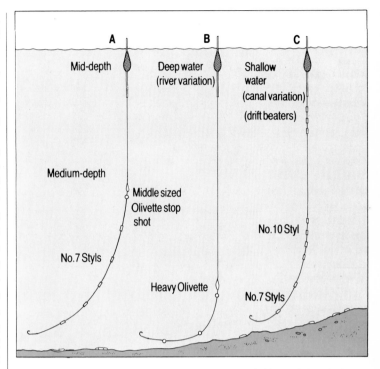

Above : Lake pole rigs.

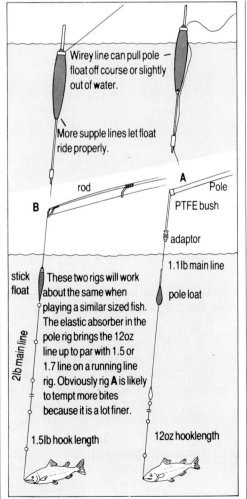

Threading a silicone buffer for Olivettes. Below left: Streamline tungsten Olivettes benefit from a silicone insert to prevent any abrasion on rough edges and to act as a buffer against the micro stop shot. First slice through the end of a length of silicone to create a taper for easy threading. Tie nylon line to the tapered end of the silicone and thread the mono through several Olivettes. Now pull the silicone through each of the weighs. **Opposite bottom:** Trim off as necessary.

In figure (Lake pole rigs):
A — Mid-depth
B — Deep water (river variation)
C — Shallow water (canal variation) (drift beaters)
Medium-depth
Middle sized Olivette stop shot
No.7 Styls
Heavy Olivette
No.10 Styl
No.7 Styls

In figure (lower diagram):
Wirey line can pull pole float off course or slightly out of water.
More supple lines let float ride properly.
rod
A — Pole
PTFE bush
adaptor
1.1lb main line
pole loat
B
stick float
2lb main line
These two rigs will work about the same when playing a similar sized fish. The elastic absorber in the pole rig brings the 12oz line up to par with 1.5 or 1.7 line on a running line rig. Obviously rig **A** is likely to tempt more bites because it is a lot finer.
1.5lb hook length
12oz hooklength

Making up pole rigs at home.

Right: This device, called a Dosapiombo makes it possible to gauge the exact weight loading required for any pole float. First clip the float inside a locking slot. Place the Dosapiombo in a container of water where it will float with the entire float standing proud of the surface. Gently drop Olivettes on the rim using tweezers or pinchers. The float will now descend to the precise depth.

Far right: Make fine adjustments using micro-shot to submerge the float's antenna by the required amount.

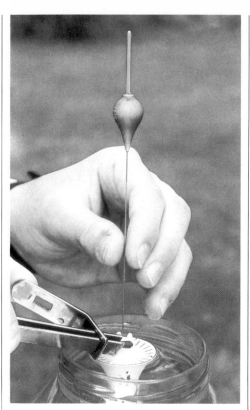

Pole fishing accessories

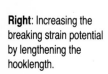

Right: Increasing the breaking strain potential by lengthening the hooklength.

or 1.7lb. It is also well suited to hooks ranging from fine wire 18s down to tiny 24s and for baits from plain maggots to casters, breadpunch, hemp, bloodworm, pinkies and squatts. If you make up 50 per cent of your pole rigs to this line on the hooklength you shouldn't go far wrong.

This leaves scope to make up some extra fine scratching rigs down to 8oz or 5oz or a few stepped up 1lb and 1.7lb bottoms for those weedy swims where a big tench or small carp might put in an appearance.

How long a hooklength?

There is quite a debate among top pole anglers as to how long a hooklength should be. The trend is to make up very short lengths down to 6in. which contradicts what most line manufacturers recommend. It's a fact that the shorter a length of fine line, the less its breaking strain becomes — because elasticity is lost.

Make your hooklengths up on the long side with a minimum of 30cm (12in) up to 1m (3ft) if you can get away with it.

Winders

Once you've made up your pole rig there are plenty of different winders available to store it on. There are extra wide winders for bodied floats and you can buy nylon clips to anchor the end of line in

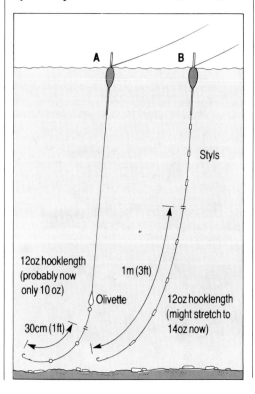

Styls

12oz hooklength (probably now only 10 oz)

1m (3ft)

Olivette

12oz hooklength (might stretch to 14oz now)

30cm (1ft)

place. For slimmer floats which fit on thinner winders, pole rig anchors are an absolute must to hold everything in place.

Never use sticky labels to anchor the end of the rig to the side of the winder. These come adrift in hot weather and make a mess of the best laid out winder trays.

Feeding aids

A small, light actioned catapult is handy for putting out squatts, pinkies and casters beyond eight metres. Another solution for spot on accuracy in flowing water is to use a small baitdropper.

The pole cup is favourite where normal groundbaiting techniques scare the fish. It consists of a small plastic open-ended cup which is fixed to the top section of the pole by a quick release clip and filled with the required feed. The pole is then manoeuvred over the fishing spot and turned over so the cup releases its contents. Excellent for feeding raw bloodworm, jokers, squatts or casters.

Rests and rollers

A good pole roller is useful because apart from making unshipping of several sections at once an easy task, it also prevents the pole from being damaged by shingle and bankside vegetation. One of the pole

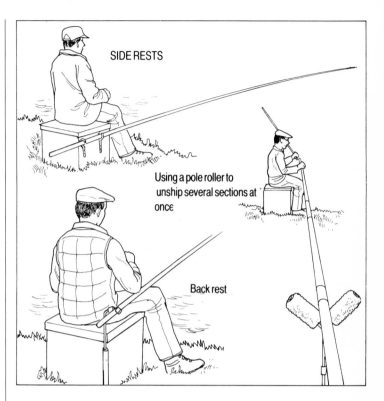

SIDE RESTS

Using a pole roller to unship several sections at once

Back rest

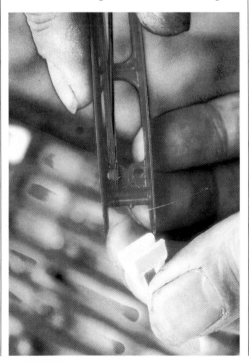

rest designs which fits to the side of the tackle box can be a good investment. You can place the pole in this type of rest while you're feeding the swim. Another useful device for taking the strain out of long pole fishing is the backrest. The extendable mini pole roller fits to the back of your tackle box.

Tackle boxes

If you are going to take up pole fishing seriously then a suitable tackle box is a priority purchase. Continental boxes are in vogue because most designs have three or four drawers or lift up trays. These are ideal for housing accessories like winders.

If possible, a box which takes attachable groundbait trays is very useful, keeping groundbait or hookbaits easily to hand. Other good accessories for the box are a fishing platform for sloping banks or adjustable legs which can be bolted to the box.

The bloodworm phenomenon

Bloodworms and their smaller cousins called jokers are banned by many clubs

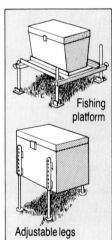

Fishing platform

Adjustable legs

Left: A nylon pole winder clip keeps everything in place without damaging fine line.

Fixed pole cup for accurate feeding right over the float.

who maintain these baits are too effective! The bloodworm is the larger bait and is used on the hook or as feed while the smaller jokers are used exclusively as feed, usually in groundbait or introduced by a bait dropper or cup. Bloodworm becomes invaluable when the fishing is extremely hard or when a cold snap in winter slows sport. It will earn bites when all else fails.

Jokers definitely activate lethargic fish and you can often put together a pleasing

net on a day when plain maggots would have failed to scrape up a single fish!

Although bloodworm is chiefly associated with small fish, it will also pick up quality roach, skimmers and even bigger tench and bream. Matchmen find the magic worm very beneficial on gin clear lakes and canals in winter and almost exclusively use it on the pole.

Feeding on the pole

Feeding is more crucial with the pole because you've got less water to play with than a running line. Normally, groundbait is the favourite baiting up method, using it as a medium to deposit small free offerings like bloodworm, jokers and squatts very accurately into the swim. Continental mixes are popular and heavy groundbaits are introduced to get feed down hard on the bottom and to disperse slowly. Several large balls of feed are often put in at the start of a session and then topped up with another couple every hour.

Drip feeding involves putting in small helpings of less stiff groundbait much more regularly, sometimes as often as every cast. In this case the groundbait should be just binding enough to reach the required distance out from the bank and should break up quickly once it hits bottom. The idea is to familiarise the fish with small balls of groundbait going in so they don't spook.

On very hard waters where groundbait can be detrimental, the method is to bind small baits into small balls with a very fine clay called leam which when dampened will put almost neat bloodworm and jokers down to the bottom without feeding the fish in any way. By using atomiser sprays, match anglers can get the consistency of this binder just right so it will even disperse into a fine cloud once it hits the water.

As a very rough guide you'll normally need to put a carpet of groundbait or feed on to the pole line to hold fish and then top up as the session progresses. Any of the feeding methods described can work or a combination — it's your job to find out which the fish prefer on the day.

Weight comparison chart

Size	Streamline	Dan Milo	Trimstyle	Conti	Lock & slide
1	0.250	0.200	...	0.200	0.200
2	0.375	0.300	0.300	0.250	0.300
3	0.500	0.500	0.400	0.350	0.400
4	0.600	0.700	0.600	0.400	0.600
5	1.000	1.000	0.800	0.600	0.800
6	1.250	1.350	1.000	0.800	1.000
7	1.500	1.500	1.200	0.900	1.200
8	1.850	...	1.500	1.250	1.500
9	2.500	...	2.000	...	2.000
10	3.150	...	...	...	2.50
11	3.750	...	...		